ANDY ANDERSON

HUNGARY 56

"We shall drag the blood-soaked Hungarian mud on to the carpets of your drawing rooms.

In vain do you take us into your homes—we still remain homeless. In vain do you dress us in new clothes—we remain in rags. From now on a hundred thousand question marks confront you.

If you wish to live in the illusion of a false peace, do not heed us. In our streets there are still cobblestones from which to build barricades. From our woods we can still get stout sticks. We still have clear consciences with which to face the guns.

But if you will heed us, listen. And at long last understand. We not only want to bear witness to the sufferings of the Hungarian people in their fight for freedom. We want to draw the attention of all people to the simple truth that freedom can only be achieved through struggle.

Peace is not simply an absence of war. No people have longed more passionately for peace than we. But it must not be the peace of quiescence. This involves complicity in oppression. We promise the world that we shall remain the apostles of freedom.

All workers, socialists, even communists, must at last understand that a bureaucratic state has nothing to do with Socialism."

Nemzetör. 15 January, 1957.

HUNGARY 56
Andy Anderson

0 948984 14 7
Phoenix Press
PO Box 824
London
N1 9DL

Printed by Little @, London

This edition of HUNGARY 56 was co-published by:-
Active Distribution
AK Press
Phoenix Press

HUNGARY 56 was first published in 1964 in Britain by the libertarian
group Solidarity. Since the early sixties Solidarity have published more
than sixty pamphlets and books, many of which are still in print. Solidarity produce the quarterly magazine Solidarity Journal, details of which
are available from:-
123 Lathom Road
London
E6 2EA

CONTENTS

Introduction

"Socialism is man's positive self-consciousness."
K. Marx. *Economic and Philosophic Manuscripts* (1844).

At 3.00 a.m. on November 4, 1956, fifteen Russian armoured divisions comprising 6,000 tanks massed at key points in Hungary to make final preparations for their second assault on a relatively defenceless people. The first assault, little more than a week earlier, had been a confused affair. Moscow pretended not to have been consulted. Hungarians had not been expected to fight the tanks almost with their bare hands. Russian soldiers had not been expected to go over to the side of the Hungarian workers in such numbers. This time, there were to be no mistakes. At 4.00 a.m. the tanks went in.

It took them nearly two weeks to crush the main centres of armed resistance. One of the greatest proletarian revolutions in history was drowned in blood. It is bitter irony indeed that those who ordered this massacre claimed to be the standard bearers of the glorious revolution of October 1917. Thirty nine years earlier, Russia had for a while been the headquarters of world revolution. From there the clarion call had gone out to the toiling and oppressed people of the world to overthrow their masters and to join hands with the Russian workers in building a new society. Today, however, it is not the midwives of the Revolution who occupy the Kremlin, it is its undertakers.

After World War II, the Russians succeeded in enforcing their 'socialism' along the banks of the Danube and up to the frontiers of Austria. They ruled an area extending from the Baltic in the north to the Balkans in the south. Over a hundred million people of various nationalities had fallen within the embrace of the new Russian bear. For many years these people had been bullied, oppressed, manipulated, managed, either by Czarist Russia or one of the Western States. Under Stalinist rule they fared no better. Their chains were if anything tightened. To them the word 'socialism' came to mean its very opposite.

In March 1953, Stalin died. In June the workers of East Berlin rebelled. The revolt, remarkable for the political character of the demands put forward, was soon quelled by Russian tanks. By 1956, these subject nations were becoming more and more of a political liability to Russia's rulers. The Russian bureaucracy recognised the danger: at the 20th Congress Krushchev himself debunked the Stalin myth and promised to liberalise Stalin's methods. But Krushchev and his supporters soon found themselves in a dilemma. It is difficult to continue practising a religion after you have destroyed its god. Although Russia's rulers attempted to break with some of the worst evils of their past, they were (and remain) incapable of coping with the root causes of these evils.

The workers of Poznan, in Poland, were the first to demonstrate what they thought of the ' changed' road to 'socialism'. The Hungarians were surprised and later elated to see how leniently these rebellious workers — and even their ' leaders '— were treated. In their turn they rose. They were victorious. And then they were crushed by the very methods Krushchev had denounced only a few months earlier. Many throughout the world were shocked at this butchery. Most of all it shocked those honest workers and intellectuals who sincerely looked to Russia as the defender of socialism. To them a treasured ideal, an ideal for which they had fought and suffered for many years, and for which many of their comrades had died, had proved to be worm-eaten.

The Hungarian Revolution was the most important event in working class history since October 1917. It marked the end of an era and the beginning of a new one. It irrevocably destroyed any moral advantage the Kremlin and those who support it may ever have had. But it was much more than this. It was a very positive event. From the Hungarian Revolution can be drawn lessons of the utmost importance for all who wish to bring about the change to a classless society in Britain or anywhere else in the world.

In 1956 the Hungarian working class inscribed on its banner the demand for workers' management of production. It insisted that Workers' Councils should play a dominant role in all realms of social life. It did so in a society in which the private ownership of the means of production (and the old ruling class based on it) had been largely eliminated. And it did so in a society in which political power was held ' on behalf of the working class ' by a self-styled working class party. In putting forward these two demands under these particular circumstances, the Hungarian workers blazed a trail. In the second half of the twentieth century their ideas will become the common heritage of all workers, in all lands.

The Hungarian Revolution was far more than a national uprising or than an attempt to change one set of rulers for another. It was a social revolution in the fullest sense of the term. Its object was a fundamental change in the relations of production, in the relations between ruler and ruled in factories, pits, and on the land. The elimination of private property in the means of production had solved none of these problems. The concentration of political power into the hands of a bureaucratic ' elite' had intensified them a thousandfold.

6

By its key demands, by its heroic example, and despite its temporary eclipse, the Hungarian Revolution upset all previous political classifications and prognoses. It created new lines of demarcation not only in the ranks of the working class movement, but in society in general. It exposed the theoretical void in the traditional 'left' A mass of old problems have now become irrelevant. Old discussions are now seen to be meaningless. The time is up for terminological subtleties, for intellectual tight-rope walking, for equivocation and for skilful avoidance of facing up to reality. For years to come all important questions for revolutionaries will boil down to simple queries: Are you for or against the programme of the Hungarian Revolution? Are you for or against workers' management of production? Are you for or against the rule of the Workers' Councils ?

Most people have only a very superficial knowledge of these weeks of October and November 1956. They have less knowledge still of the events which led up to them. We feel this book may contribute to a better knowledge and understanding of what really took place.

East-West Agreement

> ". . . From the first moment of victory, mistrust must be directed no longer against the conquered reactionary parties, but against the workers' previous allies, against the party that wishes to exploit the common victory for itself alone. . .The workers must put themselves at the command not of the State authority but of the revolutionary community councils which the workers will have managed to get adopted. . .Arms and ammunition must not be surrendered on any pretext."
> K. Marx & F. Engels. *Address to the Central Committee of the Communist League (1850).*

Prior to 1939, all the powerful capitalist nations, including Hitler's Germany, were agreed that the USSR was the real villain on the stage of history. Then the nature of their economies led them into war with one another. In 1941 Hitler invaded Russia and the western capitalist 'democracies' contracted a union with the 'villain', with the USSR. But this was no love-match. It was a marriage of expediency, coloured by the fond hope that Russia and Germany would mutually annihilate one another. Strategy was planned towards this end. But this stategy failed. The grandiose dreams of the rulers of Britain and America of emerging from the war as undisputed masters of the world did not materialise. They had reckoned without the heroic resistance of the Russian people against German fascism.

Russia paid a staggering price. The Nazi invaders caused incalculable damage to buildings and to machinery. In the early months of the war, when the Red Army was in retreat, a 'scorched earth' policy was carried out. Millions of Russians gave all they had — their very lives. Yet while the battles of World War II were still being fought the causes of World War III were already maturing.

Russia emerged from the war the second most powerful nation in the world. In throwing back the German army to the borders of the Elbe, it had acquired half a continent. These were spoils indeed and hardly the outcome bargained for by the West. Their failure to contain 'the red menace' led to near panic in their ranks.

Veiled threats were made. Two hundred thousand people were murdered in Hiroshima and Nagasaki by atom bombs. The real purpose of this crime was to warn Russia's rulers —

to show them there would be no limit to the ruthlessness[1] of the Western ruling classes should they feel their interests threatened. But the Western powers were not strong enough to challenge the situation in Europe itself. They were in no position to dispute the established fact. Eastern Europe belonged to the USSR ' by virtue of conquest '.

Formal recognition of the new reality was given at the Yalta Conference, in February 1945. Those parts of Europe ' liberated ' by the Red Army (the satellite states) would remain in the Russian sphere of influence. Western Europe and Greece would be left to Stalin's Western ' allies '. Persia was also recognised as being within the ' Western ' sphere. During the war the Red Army had ' liberated ' northern Persia. After hostilities ended, it withdrew.

With the defeat of Nazi Germany, the whole of Europe was seething for revolutionary change. Nothing like it had been felt since 1917. We shall later see how the Russian leaders maintained ' order ' in their own sphere of influence in the face of this proletarian threat to their power. In the West, the communist parties (and in some cases, the social-democratic parties) helped the ruling classes maintain their kind of order.

In FRANCE, considerable power was in the hands of Resistance groups. These were dominated by ' communists ' and ' socialists '. All that really stood between the French workers and effective power were a few shaky bayonets in the hands of British and American soldiers, most of whom only wanted to go home.

On the instructions of the Communist leaders, the Resistance groups handed over their arms to the so-called National Liberation Government headed by General de Gaulle. On January 21, 1945, Maurice Thorez, General Secretary of the French Communist Party, announced that the Patriotic Militia had served well against the Nazis. But now, he said, the situation had changed. "Public security should be assured by a regular police force. Local Committees of Liberation should not substitute themselves for the local governments."[2] His statements and actions closely resembled those of General de Gaulle.

The Communist Party was instructed to continue the campaign of wartime ' unity '. They abandoned the class struggle. They preached the virtues of production. They denounced workers defending their wages and conditions. "The strike", they said, "was the weapon of the trusts". On November 17, 1945, they entered the coalition government formed by General de Gaulle. Thorez was one of the five

1. In July 1945, the Japanese had offered to negotiate on ' unconditional surrender ' terms. They were ignored. The A-bombs were dropped on August 6 and 9. Paradoxically, the Russians were not opposed to this. They were curious to see the result : they were already working diligently to produce their own nuclear weapons.

2. Politics, *New York Times*, March 1945.

Communist leaders in a cabinet of twenty-two members. He was appointed Minister of State.

The French Communist Party's programme in 1945 can be summarised as follows: (a) control of the trusts ; (b) liberty of conscience, press and association ; (c) the right to work and leisure ; (d) social security for workers to be provided by the state ; (e) aid to the peasants through the syndicates and co-ops. Hardly the programme of a revolutionary party ! No liberal-minded Tory would have had qualms about supporting it.

In **ITALY**, the Communist leaders propped up the old ruling class in much the same way. The Communist Party, of which Togliatti was the General Secretary, had representatives in the governments of Bonomi and of Marshal Badoglio. They enthusiastically protected the capitalist state against revolution. The *New York Times* in a report during September 1944, stated : "A good many Italian fascists seek refuge in the Communist Party. Communists take over the party headquarters and institutions of the former regime like the Balila, etc., thereby soothing the transition from the old to the new.'

Nor were the ' communists ' deterred when unable to enter bourgeois coalition governments. Indeed, they helped them as much as possible by calling on the masses to support these wartime alliances. Prior to the General Election of 1945, the British Communist Party declared itself in favour of a coalition government with ' progressive ' Tories, like Eden and Churchill !

In **EASTERN EUROPE,** as we shall see, the Communists were able to gain complete control. This they did by appointing Communist ministers to take charge of the state security forces via the Ministries of the Interior. But in the West (France, Italy and Belgium) although the Communists participated in national governments[3] the Ministry of the Interior was never within their grasp. In France, Duclos reached out for this post. But the bid failed. It did not have the backing of the Red Army.

Why did these Communist Parties act in this way ? What social interests did they represent ? Had they ceased to be true parties of the working class ? The Hungarian events of 1956 were to give clear-cut answers to these questions. But already the answers were being hinted at. The Communist leaders knew that if the state machines in Western Europe were to collapse, social revolution would certainly follow. And without the backing of the Red Army, the Communists would

---

3. With the advent of Marshall Aid two years later, they were kicked out of these governments, without a word of thanks for the services they had rendered to the capitalist class.

have been powerless to control the workers.[4] While Communists have from time to time proclaimed 'all power to the workers!' they always added — if only under their breath — '... under the leadership of the Communist Party'. 'Under' is the operative word. How far under was demonstrated in Eastern Europe, from 1944 on. There they **did** have the Red Army.

---

4. That genuine revolution by the people must be avoided at all costs, was a point on which both 'communist' parties and capitalist ones were completely united.

Liberation?

**" Under Socialism all will govern in turn and will
soon become accustomed to no one governing ".
V. I. Lenin.** *The State and Revolution* (1917).

Some people still believe that the Red Army carried the
tide of social revolution with it as it entered Eastern
Europe in 1944. This is quite untrue. Not only was the
real essence of the regimes (social exploitation) left unchanged,
but for a long while even the existing political set-up was
kept in being with only a few superficial changes. Even
the same policemen were often kept on. As far as the
masses were concerned all was the same as before. Only
the language spoken by the occupying army had changed.

The reason for the Russian Government's collaboration with
the "class enemy" was, according to Molotov, "to maintain
law and order and prevent the rise of anarchy ". Rumania,
Bulgaria and Hungary provide clear examples of whose ' law '
and what ' order ' was maintained.

(a) RUMANIA

The first Eastern European state to be occupied by the Red
Army was Rumania. The Russian Government immediately
announced its intention of maintaining the status quo.

" The Soviet Government declares that it does not pursue
the aim of acquiring any part of Rumanian territory or of
changing the existing social order in Rumania. It equally
declares that the entry of Soviet troops is solely the consequence of military necessities and of the continuation of
resistance by enemy forces."[5]

The " enemy forces " were not Nazi desperadoes as might
be expected from the statement, but guerilla armies who had
been fighting the Nazis. These guerillas had originally been
organized by the Peasant Party of which the leader was Iuliu
Maniu. Maniu became a member of the new government.
When he ordered his guerillas to disband and turn in their
arms Moscow Radio commented: " Maniu's declaration is
belated. Even before this order the Red Army Command
had liquidated all bandit groups . . . "

Under the Nazis these guerillas had been ' brave resistance
fighters '. Under the Kremlin they were ' bandits '. Could
their continued resistance have been spurred on by the
composition of the new government ?

Molotov's guarantee not to interfere with the existing
social order encouraged King Michael to appoint a reactionary

5. Molotov speech of April 2, 1944.

government. General Sanatescu was made Prime Minister,[6] an office he was to hold for seven months. During this time, the workers showed what they felt. There were many uprisings and revolts against the government. The Kremlin, with an army of a million men now in the country, then decided that if Sanatescu could not control the people, he should go.

Vyshinski travelled to Bucharest. Soviet artillery was posted in front of the royal palace. This was hardly necessary. His Majesty promptly complied with Russian demands. Sanatescu's ministry was dissolved and replaced with one headed by Petru Groza.[7] Gheorghe Tatarescu became Vice-Premier.

Both Groza and Tatarescu had been members of pre-war right-wing governments. In 1911 Tatarescu had led the suppression of a peasant uprising in which 11,000 peasants had been murdered. He was Minister of State at the time of the anti-Jewish pogroms of 1927. He was world-famous as an exponent of extreme right-wing doctrines. The British Communist Party itself had called him " the leader of the Right pro-Hitler wing of the National Liberal Party ",[8] the party which helped King Carol establish his fascist regime under Marshal Antonescu.

Prime Minister Groza's government was assisted by two leading members of the Communist Party, comrades Gheorge Gheorghiu Dej and Lucretiu Patrascanu. They were allotted the respective posts of Minister of Public Works and Communications and of Minister of Justice. Patrascanu soon made his ' socialist' position clear: " Industrialists, businessmen and bankers will escape punishment as war criminals under a law being drawn up by Lucretiu Patrascanu, Minister of Justice, and Communist members of the Government. Rumania could not afford to loose the services of merchants and industrialists, M. Patrascanu said. He expressed the opinion that the country would pursue a more liberal policy towards this class than the French have ".[9]

"Premier Groza said his government did not intend to apply either collectivisation of the land or nationalisation of the banks or industries and that the mere question showed ignorance of its programme ".[10] Stalin himself advised Groza " to keep the system of private enterprise and private profit ".[11]

So, factories and enterprises owned by foreign capital were also allowed to remain intact. Capitalists who had worked

6. August 23, 1944.
7. The Kremlin's explanation to the British Government was that the Sanatescu Government was unable to maintain control over 'fascists' and ' pro-Hitlerite elements ' in the country.
8. World News and Views, November 19, 1938.
9. New York Times, March 17, 1945.
10. New York Times, September 26, 1945.
11. Radio Bucharest reported that Groza had made this statement when describing his talks with Stalin in autumn 1945.

hand-in-glove with the Nazis were permitted to keep their wealth and continue their activities. That this happened with Groza as Prime Minister is hardly surprising. He was a banker and owned many factories and a large estate. Before the war he had been a minister in two right-wing governments under General Averescu (1920-1, 1926-7).

Politically-conscious Rumanian workers did not expect such a government to represent interests other than those of the big landowners and financiers. Nor did they wonder why Groza was openly opposed to measures of social reform and why he staunchly upheld the sanctity of private property. But that a government carrying out a policy of suppressing workers and peasants should have been virtually appointed by Soviet Russia forced many Rumanian revolutionaries to think. It forced them to change opinions and ideals they had held for years. Eventually, even Maniu and his supporters withdrew from Parliament. But such were the rumblings among the people that even this trivial demonstration of independence could not be tolerated by the government and its Communist supporters. Maniu was promptly charged with being 'anti-monarchist',[12] a 'fascist' and an 'enemy of the people'.

Maniu was tried and sentenced to solitary confinement for life.[13] The President of the tribunal was the wartime Director General of prisons and concentration camps. He owed his appointment to the tribunal to a leading member of the Communist Party, Patrascanu.

(b) **BULGARIA**

When the Red Army occupied Bulgaria the Russian-backed 'Fatherland Front' Government took over. It was headed by Colonel Khimon Georgiev. Colonel Demain Velchev was Minister of War. Both had been former leaders of the Military League, a fascist organisation sponsored by Mussolini.[14]

Colonel Georgiev had also been the instigator of the fascist coup of 1934 which had dismissed Parliament, dissolved the unions and declared them illegal. He had then become Prime Minister and had begun a reign of terror which, in its ruthless ferocity, surpassed even that of 1923. The Minister of the Interior of the new 'Fatherland Front' Government was Anton Yugow, a Communist leader. He controlled the state security forces and was responsible for maintaining

---

12. At an election meeting in Bucharest on November 17, 1946, Gheorghiu Dej (leader of the Communist Party) ended his speech with the slogans: " Vote for the King's government ! Long live the King ! Long live his commanders and soldiers ! Long live the Army which is his and the people's ! " [Ygael Gluckstein, *Stalin's Satellites in Europe*, Allen & Unwin, p.141.]
13. Maniu died in 1955.
14. In 1923, the Military League organised a *coup d'état* and overthrew the progressive regime of Stambulinski. Stambulinski was assassinated. Tens of thousands of his supporters, together with many Communists and socialists, were murdered.

' order '.

When the Nazi military machine eventually collapsed, the great majority of the Bulgarian people were naturally overjoyed. Although tired of war and oppression, their relief did not lead them to inactivity. Revolution—the opportunity at last to become the masters of their own destiny — now appeared possible. During the autumn months of 1944, in Sofia and other towns, workers' militias arrested the fascists and clamped them in gaol. They held mass demonstrations. They elected full democratic people's tribunals. The police were disarmed and in many cases disbanded.

The soldiers' feelings were in harmony with those of the people: " Reports on the Bulgarian forces of occupation in Western Thrace and Macedonia vividly recall the picture of the Russian Army in 1917. Soldiers' councils have been set up. Officers have been degraded, red flags hoisted, and normal saluting has been abolished."[15] This similarity to 1917 was anathema to the Russian and Bulgarian ' Communist ' leaders. Backed by the Russian High Command, the Minister of War, Colonel Velchev, issued a strict order to his troops. " Return immediately to normal (sic) discipline. Abolish Soldiers' Councils. Hoist no more red flags."

Sincere Bulgarian Communists denounced the hypocrisy of the Russians. Molotov attempted to quell the ensuing furore: " If certain Communists continue their present conduct, we will bring them to reason. Bulgaria will remain with her democratic government and her present order . . . You must retain all valuable army officers from before the coup d'etat. You should reinstate in the service all officers who have been dismissed for various reasons."[16]

The sinister ring of these words echoed through Bulgaria. In 1934, the fascist Colonel Georgiev had attacked the workers. He had suppressed strikes with loss of life and declared them illegal. In 1945, the same Colonel Georgiev, now a Communist stooge, attacked striking workers as ' fascists.' " In March 1945 a number of coal miners struck for higher wages. They were immediately branded as ' anarchists ' and ' fascists ', and rushed into jail by the Communist-controlled state militia."[17]

(c) **HUNGARY**

In 1918, the feeling in Hungary had been strong for revolutionary change. These feelings had for a time been peacefully channelled through the Government of Count Karolyi, who had a reputation for being some kind of a Socialist. The Karolyi Government made *some* concessions to the people. In March 1919, the Allies brought about the fall of the Karolyi Government. They issued Hungary with an ultimatum concerning the frontier with Czechoslovakia

15. *The Economist*, October 7, 1944.
16. *New York Times*, January 16, 1945.
17. *The Nation*, June 23, 1945.

which Hungarians felt would be ' crippling the cripple '.
Patriotic and revolutionary feelings combined and Bela
Kun's[18] Government rode in on the crest of a new revolutionary wave. Communists dominated the new administration, although it contained a number of Social Democrats.
In March 1919, the new government proclaimed the
Hungarian Soviet Republic. This was not imposed on the
country by a Russian army. There was no direct contact
between Hungary and Russia. Russia had quite enough to
contend with at this time.

Prisoners of war returning from Russia gave accounts,
excitedly and with undisguised admiration, of the Great
Revolution, news of which inspired the people with hope for
a new way of life. How badly the Hungarians needed to
cling to such a hope !

Hungary was a predominantly peasant country in which
the distribution of land was more unjust than in any other
part of Europe. Almost all the land was owned by
aristocrats and by the Church. The majority of the people
were landless, unemployed and close to starvation. To end
the feudal land structure at this time would have been a
truly revolutionary act.

Bela Kun's Government lasted a little over four months.
Some argue there was no time for such measures. But
not even the promise was made. Had such steps been taken,
Bela Kun's regime might have lasted longer. It would have
been difficult, if not impossible, for successive governments
to take the land away from the peasants again, without facing
the prospect of prolonged civil war. As it was, the Kun
regime was overthrown as soon as the Rumanian Army had
occupied Budapest. Bela Kun fled to Russia on August 1,
1919.[19]

The demise of the Kun Government had been planned at
Szeyed by Admiral Nicholas Horthy and his supporters.
Representatives of the Rumanian Army had been present. A
White Terror was let loose on Hungary by Horthy's foreign-
assisted counter-revolution. The first fascist regime in
Europe was set up. For the Hungarians, all former horrors
were now surpassed. Thousands of Communists and
Socialists were rounded up by fascist gangs, beaten, tortured,
killed. The Trade Unions were violently suppressed. Those

18. Kun was Foreign Minister, but he dominated the Government.
19. Kun opposed Stalin during the great purges of the middle thirties
and was executed. In February 1962 a national delegate conference of
Kadar's Hungarian Journalists' Union ' cleared ' Kun's name. The
Union's President, Dr. Arpad Szakasits, paid high tributes to Kun, his
'' great central committee,'' and his *Voros Utsag*—the first Hungarian
Communist newspaper. It was also reported (Feb. '62) that Bela Kun's
widow and son, who live on a farm in the Soviet Union, had been invited
by Kadar to return and settle in Hungary. (Szakasits was an ex-Social
Democratic leader and editor of *Nepszava* in 1944. He succeeded Tildy
as President of Hungary in 1948. Became a victim of Rakosi's ' Salami
tactics' (see Chapter 4) and was imprisoned for four years.)

merely suspected of socialist sympathies were tortured and finally murdered. Thousands of people, quite unconnected with such ideas, suffered persecution and death. So frightful were the reports of atrocities that even the British (who knew all about atrocities in India) were moved to send a Parliamentary Commission to Budapest. The Commission reported that "the worst stories of mutilation, rape, torture and murder" were proved.

The activities of the Hungarian Communist Party at this time are referred to by Peter Fryer in his book *Hungarian Tragedy*: "The tiny Communist Party carried out its work in deep illegality. It made the kind of sectarian mistakes that are so easy to make under such conditions, with leaders in jail and murdered" (p.29). The movement was 'decapitated' and floundered. This is inevitable under conditions of civil war, whenever revolutionary movements are obsessed with the cult of leadership. It is a pre-requisite of success under such conditions, that the leading activities of a movement be spread as far and wide as possible throughout its membership. No one should be indispensable. Arrested 'leaders' should always be replaceable by others.

For the Hungarian people the following years under Horthy's fascist tyranny were full of dread and suffering. Some people have claimed that Horthy's regime was not truly fascist. But we must remember that fascism in power may take a variety of forms. Although basically similar, the regimes of Hitler, Mussolini, Franco and Salazar also differed in several particulars. Perhaps Horthy's regime could best be called 'rule by aristocratic fascists'. Whatever its name, its sickening bestiality, as far as the ordinary people were concerned, remains as a scar on the body of humanity.

The Horthy regime took part in World War II on Hitler's side. However towards the end of this war a movement developed which sought to detach Hungary from its alliance with Nazi Germany. Nazi troops then occupied the country and the terror ruled again. Left-wing militants were ruthlessly hunted out and exterminated. Some 400,000 Hungarian Jews were deported to agony and death in Nazi concentration camps.

Despite this long history of misery, the Hungarian people had not given up their hope of a better life. When in 1944 the Red Army began to occupy the country the people were well disposed towards it. They sincerely held Russia to be a friend. They trusted the promise of liberation. Many Russians had given their lives in bitter battles to drive out the German Nazis. The glorious ideals of 1917 were not forgotten. So trusting were the few Hungarian Communists that they helped to organise the dividing up of large estates among the peasants.

In December 1944, a Hungarian government was formed at Debrecen in the Russian-occupied area. A shudder went through the people. The First Minister was the Hungarian

17

Commander-in-Chief General Bela Miklos de Dolnok. Bela Miklos had been the first Hungarian personally to receive from Hitler the greatest Nazi honour : Knight Grand Cross of the Iron Cross. Only a few months earlier, in July 1944, General Bela Miklos had held the highly trusted job of messenger between the principal organiser of the White Terror, Admiral Horthy, and the vilest Nazi of them all, Adolf Hitler.[20]

There were two other generals in the Government : Vörös and Faragho. General Janos Vörös, Bela Miklos's ex-Chief-of-Staff, became Minister for Defence. Imre Nagy became the Minister for Agriculture. The rest of the Government was formed of members of the Communist, Social Democratic and Smallholders parties. The *Economist* described it at the time as " a queer collection of the local denizens and the parties of the left ".

The new government still considered Admiral Horthy the legitimate ruler of Hungary. The Minister for Defence, General Vörös, ended his first speech over the Russian radio with the contradictory slogan: "Long live a free and democratic Hungary, under the leadership of Admiral Horthy!". The first declaration of the Russian-sponsored government as broadcast by Moscow radio on December 24, 1944, proclaimed : " The Regent of our country, Nicholas Horthy, has been seized by the Germans. The mercenaries now in Budapest[21] are usurpers. The country has been left without leadership at a moment when the reins of government must be taken in strong hands . . . Vital interests of the nation demand that the armed forces of the Hungarian peoples, together with the Soviet Union and democratic peoples, should help in the destruction of Hitlerism. The Provisional Government declares that it regards private property as the basis of economic life and the social order of the country and will guarantee its continuity ".

General Miklos, Knight Grand Cross of the Iron Cross, had read the proclamation. It sounds incredible. How could such a man call for " the destruction of Hitlerism "? To people like Bela Miklos, the privileges, prestige and power that go with leadership, were the paramount considerations. The nature of the leadership, its policy, methods and aims, were of secondary consequence. But how could Soviet Russia put such men into leading positions ? The main reason was given by Miklos himself in the declaration quoted above : " . . . The country has been left without leadership . . . ". In other words a political vacuum existed. There was a real danger of it being filled by the organisations thrown up by the industrial and agricultural workers. The workers had taken Communist propaganda at its face value. They had already begun to act upon it. This was extremely dangerous

---

20. See *Admiral Nicholas Horthy—Memoirs*, p.222.
21. At this time the Germans still occupied the capital. They fought in every street, leaving a devastated city behind them.

for the Soviet leadership and for all those who accepted it. The only people the Russians could rely on were the remnants of the previous ruling groups.

Russian beliefs that nobody other than erstwhile managers and administrators could run the country were not new. The seeds had been sown in Russia itself, shortly after the October Revolution and long before the Stalin era. Prior to the Revolution the Bolsheviks had repeatedly advocated workers' control of production. But as early as the spring of 1918 — and long before the difficulties imposed by the Civil War — leading Party members were stressing the advantages of 'one-man management' of industry. They were soon actively denouncing those within their own Party — and those outside it — who still held to the view that only collective management could be a genuine basis for socialist construction.

We cannot here deal with this extremely important and complex period of working class history, nor with the extremely tense controversies which this question of management gave rise to.[22] There can be little doubt however that it is in the events, difficulties and conflicts of *this* period that one should seek the real roots of the degeneration of the Russian Revolution. Many years later, even the bourgeoisie was to perceive the significance of what then took place. When *The Guardian*[23] refers to Lenin's writings of March 1918 as "dealing in part with emulating capitalist organisation of industry within a socialist framework", it is merely expressing this awareness with its customary mixture of naivete and sophistication.

The dangers that would flow from such ideas had been clearly perceived in Russia by a grouping known as the Workers Opposition. As early as 1921, one of its prominent members, Alexandra Kollontai, had written : "Distrust towards the working class (not in the sphere of politics, but in the sphere of economic creative abilities) is the whole essence of the theses signed by our Party leaders. They do not believe that the rough hands of workers, untrained technically, can mould these economic forms which in the passage of time shall develop into a harmonious system of Communist production.

" To all of them—Lenin, Trotsky, Zinoviev and Bukharin —it seems that production is such a ' delicate thing ' that it is impossible to get along without the assistance of ' managers '. First of all, we shall ' bring up ' the workers, ' teach them '. Only when they grow up shall we remove from them all the teachers of the Supreme Council of National Economy and let the industrial unions take control over production. It is significant that all the theses written by the

22. For further information on this subject see *Solidarity* Pamphlet No. 7, *The Workers Opposition*, by Alexandra Kollontai.
23. *The Guardian*, September 29, 1962.

Party leaders coincide on this essential point : for the present we shall not give the trade unions control over production. For the present, 'we shall wait'. They all agree that at present the management of production must be carried on over the workers' heads by means of a bureaucratic apparatus inherited from the past."[24]

In the capitalist West, of course, there had never been any 'nonsense' about the workers controlling and managing production. When the Western powers 'liberated' parts of Europe in 1945, the Military Governments set up by the occupying armies ensured that only people with a particular social background or a particular kind of previous experience were put or retained in commanding managerial or administrative positions.[25] To the victors it mattered little to what ends—or to whose ends—this experience had been put in the past. Like spoke to like—and they got on fine ! The mystique of management cut across national boundaries.

As it became obvious that the future rulers of Hungary would be the Communist Party and its rapidly forming bureaucracy, the place-seeking elements came flocking in. The Party became the recruiting centre for the future 'leaders' and managers. (A similar process had occurred in Germany, with the rise of Hitler's party.) Economic administration and political rule were concentrated into fewer and fewer hands.

24. *Solidarity* Pamphlet No. 7, *The Workers Opposition*, by Alexandra Kollontai, p.20.

25. The author, who was a P.O.W. in Austria and remained there for six months after the war had ended, has personal experience of all this.
    While working with American Intelligence in Styria, he was arrested on the order of the American Military Governor of the area. He was again put behind barbed wire in an ex-P.O.W. camp in the town of Stainach. An American guard was placed over the camp. Two American members of the Intelligence Unit were also arrested, but were not seen again by Anderson, who escaped from the camp the very same night and went into hiding.
    Anderson and the others had been actively objecting to leading local Nazis being retained in or given positions of authority by the American Military Government. When the British took over this particular zone from the Americans, Anderson came out of hiding and joined a British Intelligence Unit operating from the town of Liezen. Things were no better. The British Military Government also regarded the strutting Nazi administrators and managers of only a few weeks earlier as the only people they could rely on. A similar situation developed as with the American Military Government. Anderson was again arrested.

Salami and Reparations

"An intelligent victor will, whenever possible, present his demands to the vanquished in instalments."
A. Hitler. *Mein Kampf* (1925).

In the East European states, the systematic destruction of the Socialist and Peasant parties began gently. It continued with increased tempo until, by 1948, they had been virtually liquidated. It was essential that no means of opposition be open to the people if the tools of the Russian bureaucracy, the national Communist parties, were to carry out their programmes.

The people were already beginning to feel that their trust in Soviet Russia was being betrayed. There is no more bitter and painful disappointment than that caused when a friend betrays your trust. The Hungarian Communists knew this. They knew what passions it would arouse. They were only a minority. Their ruthless determination to hold on to power had to be made apparent to all.

Their instrument of repression was of course the police. Complete control of this force was essential. By gaining the key post of the Ministry of Interior, this was assured them. Through this Ministry they also controlled the Civil Service. All the key positions were held by their members. The party of the proletariat, far from destroying the existing state machine, utilised it and strengthened it to establish its dictatorship *over* the proletariat. In later describing their methods, Rakosi said that in those days the very idea of the dictatorship of the proletariat was discussed only in limited Party circles. "We did not bring (it) before the Party publicly because even the theoretical discussion of the Dictatorship of the Proletariat as an objective, would have caused alarm among our companions in the coalition. It would have made more difficult our endeavour to win over . . . the majority of the mass of the workers."[26]

The winning over of the workers to a revolutionary programme would have been only too easy. But the Party would have lost control of the workers in the process. In their fear of this, the Party united with their bourgeois ' companions in the coalition '.

Rakosi explained how the ' Revolution ' had been made from above and how it had brought the Hungarian Communist

---

26. From Rakosi's speech of February 29, 1952, to the Party Academy (see *The Road of our People's Democracy*, published in June 1952 by the Hungarian News and Information Service).

Party to power. He described how, through the Ministry of the Interior, the Party had been able to 'unmask' the leaders of the Smallholders Party, 'reveal' their crimes and 'remove' them. Rakosi described how the opposition was cut into slices (like a salami sausage) and discarded. " In those days this was called 'salami tactics' . . . We sliced off, bit by bit, reaction in the Smallholders Party . . . We whittled away the strength of the enemy."[26]

Rakosi also described the fusion of the Communist Party with the Social Democratic Party as a complete victory for the Communists and utter defeat for the Social Democrats. (How easy this must have been, with the Minister of the Interior to reveal the 'crimes' of the Social Democrats !) He then related how the Communist Party 'captured' the army, police and state security forces (i.e. the secret police). This was achieved in " bitter battle . . . the more so because our Party already had a strong foothold in those organisations . . . When in the autumn of 1948, our Party took over the Ministry of Defence, the vigorous development of the defence forces could start."[26]

That the absolute control of the secret police is indispensable to those who wish to suppress the people, was also made quite clear by Rakosi himself. " There was one position, control of which was claimed by our Party from the first minute. One position where the Party was not inclined to consider any distribution of the posts according to the strength of the parties in the coalition. This was the State Security Authority . . . We kept this organisation in our hands from the first day of its establishment."[26] The leaders of the Communist Party knew exactly what they were doing when they took control of the A.V.O. (Secret Security Police).

The Hungarian secret police used all the latest techniques of torture and murder known to the Gestapo and N.K.V.D. Soviet occupation troops had been immediately followed into Hungary by the 'political experts' of the N.K.V.D., who immediately proceeded to 'reorganise' the security forces. These were now staffed by a curious mixture of the old vermin of the Horthy regime and the new scum of the Communist Party. This human garbage occupied a privileged position in Hungarian society. The national average wage in 1956 was about 1,000 forints a month. The pay of A.V.O. 'rankers' was 3,000 forints a month. Officers were paid between 9,000 and 12,000 forints a month. All were passionately hated by the Hungarian people.

The ' salami tactics ' of taking over the State apparatus evoked criticism from a number of Communist Party members. The ' leadership ' dealt with their critics . . . through the police. The Party was directly responsible for the terror, the murder, the torture and the beatings which were a feature of Hungarian life under the Rakosi regime.

* * *

Along with violent political suppression, the workers also suffered the slower agony of deteriorating economic standards, amounting at times to starvation. The reparation payments extracted by Russia accounted for this to no small degree.

The reparations plot was hatched at the Yalta Conference, where the West had agreed with Stalin to carve up Europe into spheres of influence. After World War I the Soviet Union had vigorously condemned the reparations exacted from Germany by the victorious Allies through the Treaty of Versailles. It continually and correctly emphasised that these extortions placed an intolerable burden upon the German working class who were not responsible for the war and for the damage it had caused. At the time, the same opinions had been clearly and firmly voiced by the various national Communist Parties. During World War II, as the hopes of a Russian victory grew brighter, this line was dropped. It looked as if the Russians might be on the receiving end of reparations. The chameleon ideology of their ' socialism ' showed itself. What was deemed ' robbery ' by the capitalist states became ' justice ' when the Russians practised it.

Exact figures as to the quantity of machinery, etc., dismantled and sent to the U.S.S.R. are not available. One estimate for Hungary puts it at 124 million dollars. Like Hitler's army, the Red Army lived off the country it occupied. Here again exact figures for these occupation costs are lacking. However, an addition to the country's population of over a million men must have used up a great deal of the nation's food produce alone. A rather hypocritical American note to the Russian Government, dated July 23, 1946, stated that " the Soviet Forces had, up to June 1945, taken out of Hungary four million tons of wheat, rye, barley, maize and oats. (The total pre-war annual production of these grains was a little over 7 million tons.) Of the foodstuffs available for the urban population in the second half of 1945, the Soviet Army had appropriated nearly all the meat, one sixth of the wheat and rye, one quarter of the legumes, nearly three quarters of the lard, a tenth of the vegetable oils and a fifth of the milk and dairy products. Extensive requisitioning of food was going on as late as April 1946." The food shortage during this period was so serious that each person was getting at the most only 850 calories a day — less than in Germany or Austria. As one might expect, the increase in the death rate was alarming.

Another unknown quantity is the amount of material (personal goods, etc.) which found its way to Russia through looting.

The known list of reparations extracted from Eastern Europe is staggering enough. We cannot here go into the details for each country. Some details about Hungary should give a picture of the whole.

The total reparations demands from Hungary amounted to 300 million dollars. Two-thirds of this went to Russia and the rest was divided equally between Czechoslovakia and Yugoslavia. Industrial goods constituted 83% of the total. The remaining 17% was agricultural products. Before the war, industrial products made up only about a quarter of all Hungarian exports. The British parliamentary delegation which visited Hungary in the spring of 1946, stated that the combined costs of reparations and of the occupation amounted to 30% of the national income (reparations 18%, occupation 12%). A U representative at the October 1946 session of the Paris Peace Conference had put these costs at 35% of the national income.

The scale of these reparations placed an enormous burden on the Hungarian economy and hence on the producers: the working class. By 1948, despite the A.V.O. and the Red Army, their resentment might have erupted into the streets. The danger was reported to the Kremlin. In July 1948 Russia decided to waive half the reparations still due. On December 15, 1948, the Finance Minister, Erno Gerö, was able to tell the Hungarian Parliament that, although in 1948, 25.4% of the national expenditure went to pay Russian reparations, only 9.8% of the budget for 1949 would be allocated to this purpose.

Methods of Exploitation and Subjugation

" Masses of labourers, crowded into the factory, are organized like soldiers. As privates of the industrial army, they are placed under the command of a perfect hierarchy of officers and sergeants."
K. Marx and F. Engels. *The Communist Manifesto* (1848).

(a) TRADE.

There were still other ways of exploiting the people. Trade, for example. The Communist governments of Eastern Europe soon saw that Russian heavy industry was incapable of providing them with capital goods. They knew that machinery and raw materials were essential. They were prepared to try and get these from the West. The Marshall Plan seemed to be an answer to the problem. At least two of these countries, Czechoslovakia and Poland, made clear their desire to take part in the Marshall Plan. Even after pressure from Moscow had compelled them to drop the idea, attempts were still made to get trade with the West.

Moscow's plans in this period were helped by Washington. The U.S.A. established an ' iron curtain ' to trade between the West and the countries of Eastern Europe, when she instructed other Western nations not to export ' strategic goods '. The State Department's ' secret list ' of strategic goods covered practically every kind of capital equipment. It included such items as gramophone recording discs and needles for the textile industry.[27] Trade with the Soviet Union (on Russia's terms) was assured.

To some people, the term ' trade ' means ' a mutually agreed exchange of commodities between countries '. Those in the Kremlin did not accept this definition. Their idea of trade was based on the old imperialist principle of buying cheap and selling dear — very, very dear !

The satellite states were regarded as a source of raw materials and of cheap manufactured goods. Exploitation worked in two directions. Russia secured the satellites' exports at below world prices. And it exported to them at

---

27. See speech by the Polish Foreign Minister Modzelewski, to a Committee of the U.N. General Assembly (November 2, 1948).

above world prices. The Polish—Soviet agreement of August 16, 1945, for the annual export of Polish coal to the U.S.S.R. is a startling example. " The robbery of Poland through this transaction alone amounted to over one hundred million dollars a year. British capitalists never got such a large annual profit out of their investments in India."[28] Shoes manufactured in Czechoslovakia at a cost of 300 crowns a pair were sold to Russia at 170 crowns a pair. Yet when the Czech government, owing to the severe drought of 1947, was forced to import large quantities of grain from the U.S.S.R., it had to pay more than 4 dollars a bushel for it. At the time, the U.S.A. was selling grain at 2.5 dollars per bushel on the world market.

Bulgaria found no difficulty in selling her tobacco for badly needed dollars. Yet in 1948, she had to sell nearly all her tobacco crop to the U.S.S.R. at a very low price. Russia was then able to re-sell the tobacco to Italy, making a handsome profit — in dollars.

That Russian ' trade ' with Hungary was considerable is shown by the 1948 long-term agreement. This stated that ' trade ' was to be trebled in 1949. No details were given. Although Russia supplied cotton, and Hungary manfactured goods, the quantities involved and their prices were as jealously guarded as military secrets. One of the main reasons for the secrecy was that workers in the factories were, to some extent, aware of this exploitation and strongly resented it.

(b) **MIXED COMPANIES.**

The amount of German capital invested in Bulgaria, Hungary and Rumania, was considerable. In Rumania, for example, it equalled over a third of all investments in oil, banking and industry. In Hungary, German-owned property was estimated at being worth 1,200 million dollars. Russia exercised her ' rights ' under the Potsdam agreement. All German investments were confiscated. (The Russians only took over the assets of the various enterprises. Their liabilities were charged to the state.) This was done partly by dismantling machinery, partly by taking control of those industries still operating in Hungary. Jointly controlled companies were set up. These were, at first, operated in partnership with private capitalists but when these were later expropriated, the U.S.S.R. held joint control of the companies with the Hungarian Government.[29] No industry was completely owned by the U.S.S.R. Russia invested in as many undertakings as possible, thus gaining a greater grip over the whole economy. These ' mixed companies ' were organized and conducted on capitalist lines. The only notable difference was that one side of the ' equal ' partnership

28. Ygael Gluckstein—*Stalin's Satellites in Europe* (p.66)—an excellent source of information for the period up to 1950.
29. Similar developments occurred in Bulgaria, Poland, Rumania and Czechoslovakia.

(U.S.S.R.) was making far greater profits than the other (the satellite State). In some cases the latter even had to underwrite the losses !

(c) NATIONALIZATION.

It was not, however, until 1948 that integration of the Hungarian economy into that of the Soviet Union was seriously begun. This was achieved through nationalization.

The term ' nationalization ', when used by the leaders of either East or West, has only one meaning : to ensure and consolidate their own control over the means of distribution. production and exchange.[30]

In Hungary, some industries had already been nat:onalized. But until the nationalization law of March 25, 1948, 25% of heavy industry and 80% of all other industry was still in private hands. This law laid down that all firms employing more than 100 people were to be taken over by the State.

It was not until the end of 1949 that nationalization was completed. The Hungarian Communist leaders did not differ from those of the British Labour Party on the question of whether nationalization. should involve control by the workers themselves. This is shown by the report that "Easter Monday, 1948, was declared a holiday. While the workers were not in the factories, State officials came down and took them over. The next day the workers arrived to find a new master ".[31] Nationalization by the Labour Government was carried out with rather more political sophistication. As far as the workers were concerned, the net result was much the same.[32]

(d) COLLECTIVIZATION.

Another method of exploiting the population was the Russian type of collectivization. While in other states of

---

30. Lord Chandos, chairman of Associated Electrical Industries, and head of the Institute of Directors, said at a luncheon of the Coal Industry Society at the Hyde Park Hotel, in London, on January 8. 1962 : " Nationalization of a fairly substantial sector of industry has come to stay. . . It is quite clear that every loyal citizen must try to make our nationalized industries work efficiently. I congratulate Lord Robens (ex-front bench Labour M.P.) Chairman of the National Coal Board, on having many ideas. I congratulate the coal trade upon the lively revival in marketing. As an industrialist I want cheap fuel and reliable supplies and I believe that is what you will secure for us." (*The Guardian,* January 9, 1962).

31. *Continental News Service,* April 16, 1948.

32. Another similarity between the Hungarian (or any other) Communist Party and the British (or any other) Labour Party is that both profess to be parties of the working class. Both no doubt started with the objective of ' emancipating labour '. Both have become obstacles to this end. Both are now the mouthpieces of non-proletarian strata. In their internal organization—and in their conceptions of their relations to the masses—both now reflect the fundamental division of exploiting society into order-givers and order-takers. Objectively, the function of both types of party is to force the working class to accept a 'rationalised' form of exploitation.

Eastern Europe this was begun at an early stage, in Hungary, the Government remained, for a long time, shy at making the attempt. After some manoeuvring, it eventually began slowly to 'collectivize' agriculture.

By November 1949, some 7% of the arable land was in the hands of co-operative or state farms. The diffidence of the Hungarian rulers was due mainly to their fear of open opposition from the agricultural workers. The reason, in the jargon of the government, was that faster collectivization might strengthen 'Titoist tendencies'.

In the process of completing nationalization, what few rights the workers had enjoyed under private ownership were whittled away. Strikes, as before, were of course illegal. Complete control of the factory was placed in the hands of a single manager. Minister Erno Gerö, in his June 1950 report to the Central Committee of the Party, put it like this : " a factory . . . can have only one manager who in his own person is responsible for everything that happens in the factory ". The screw subjecting the workers to the will of management had been given the final turn. Hungary was a fully qualified satellite of the U.S.S.R.

The destruction of the gains which the Russian workers had for a short while secured in 1917 had taken rather longer. True, the Party campaign for ' one man management ' of product'on — and against workers' management — had begun as early as the spring of 1918. It met with considerable resistance. For the first few years industries were run by the so-called Troika, i.e. the workers' committee, the Party cell and the manager. By 1924 even this had become a farce. By 1929 the Party's Central Committee felt ready to pass a resolution that workers' factory committees " may not intervene directly in the running of the plant or endeavour in any way to replace plant management. They shall, by all means possible, help to secure one-man control, increased production, plant development and thereby improve the material conditions of the working class."[33]   The ghost of the erstwhile Troika was not officially buried until 1937. The official presiding at this particular ceremony was Stalin's right-hand man, Zhdanov. Speaking at the Plenum of the Central Committee he said: " . . . the Troika is something quite impermissible . . . the Troika is a sort of administrative board, but our economic administration is conducted along totally different lines."[34]

In the 'workers' states ' of Eastern Europe, the people were not even allowed to go through these limited and distorted forms of economic self-administration. The Troika system was never introduced.

Given the complete political and economic integration with the Soviet Union, nothing seemed now to stand in the way of total exploitation. Nothing ?

33. *Pravda*, September 7, 1929.
34. *Pravda*, March 11, 1937.

Resistance Grows

"Piece-wage is the form of wages most in harmony with the capitalist mode of production . . . it served as a lever for lengthening the working day and the lowering of wages."
K. Marx. *Capital* (1867).
"It has been the iron principle of the National Socialist leadership not to permit any rise in the hourly wage rates but to raise income solely by an increase in performance."
A. Hitler, speaking at the Party Congress of Honour.
"Piece-work is a revolutionary system that eliminates inertia and makes the labourer hustle. Under the capitalist system loafing and laziness are fostered. But now, everyone has a chance to work harder and earn more."
Scanteia [Rumanian Communist daily]. January 13, 1949.

The ' chance to work harder '—through piece-work—was introduced into Hungary on an unprecedented scale. Piece-work appeals to the baser instincts of man. This is apparent in our own society. Piece-work is much praised by those who rule us. For the managers of the people, here or abroad, it is an important means of controlling, manipulating and dominating the workers. Piece-work helps break up their natural tendency to unite and cooperate. It is a valuable weapon in the hands of those who wish to demoralize and atomize the working class.

The whole piece-work system depends upon basic wages being kept at a low level. In Poland, for example, because of the extent of piece-work, basic wages almost disappeared. The system was bolstered by the Russian-style Stakhanovites. These were the piece-workers, par excellence. The type exists in British factories and they are usually disliked. The workers in Eastern Europe were quite hostile to them. The Stakhanovites themselves continually complained of this hostility. The official party organs deplored it as an " attack on Stakhanovites by politically immature workers ". In fact, the 9th congress of the Czechoslovak Communist Party called for measures against these workers " who run down the work of the Stakhanovites and who even try to put a spoke in their wheel."

In Hungary, not only the workers, but even some Party members, were trying to put a spoke in the wheel of the whole piece-work system. In a speech on November 27, 1948,

Rakosi referred to this and to various 'go-slow' movements among the workers when he said: "... the factory directors are capitulating to the lazy workers. The production quotas are too low". But although the 'lazy workers' were being continually threatened, they did not mend their ways. In June, 1950, Erno Gerö, in his report to the Party's Central Committee, declared : " wage and norm swindling have spread among the masses. They can be attributed, to a great degree, to the underground work of right-wing social-democratic elements and their allies, the clerical reactionaries. That such an unsavoury situation in the field of norms could arise is partly because, in many cases, the economic leaders of the factories, Party functionaries and trade union members, are among those who slacken the norms . . . In more than one case they go so far as to protect and support the wage swindlers ". Having virtually stated that Party members were in league with 'right-wing Social Democrats', Gerö arranged for a big increase in the basic norm.

Conditions in the factories worsened. On January 9, 1950, the Hungarian Government issued a decree prohibiting workers from leaving their place of work without permission. Penalties for disobeying were severe.[35]

Increasing alienation and exploitation in any country in the world are invariably met by increasing resistance. Sabotage becomes widespread. This is one of the economic facts of life. It is well known to all industrial sociologists and is openly discussed by those of them who are not directly in the pay of the giant corporations.[36]

That Hungarian workers *were* resisting became even clearer through the utterances of their 'leaders'. Speaking at Debrecen on December 6, 1948, the Hungarian Minister of Industry, Istvan Kossa,[37] said: " The workers have assumed a terrorist attitude towards the directors of the nationalized industries ". He added that if they didn't change their attitude, a spell of forced labour might help. Workers who didn't seem to be in love with their work were often denounced by the leaders as 'capitalist agents'.

Despite police terror, workers found several ways of resisting. The two most important were absenteeism and turning out work of poor quality. On August 31, 1949, Rakosi stated that production had fallen " by 10 - 15% in the last few months ". He also claimed that the number of days

---

35. Although there is an almost monastic silence about them, forced labour camps certainly existed in Hungary. An indication of their existence was given on August 21, 1950, when Radio Budapest reported that I. Olagos, a worker in the wagon factory at Györ, had been found guilty of a 'wages swindle' and sentenced to six years compulsory labour.

36. See *Solidarity*, vol. II, No. 1, p.15 "Who Sabots ? "

37. Kossa was a former Budapest tramworkers' leader who had been sent with a penal labour battalion to the Russian front, captured by the Red Army and 'politically educated' at a Russian training centre. He became boss of the Communist-reorganized trade unions, in 1945.

lost due to workers going sick was 2 to 3 times higher than before the war.[38] *The Times* (September 5, 1949) carried a report from its Budapest correspondent on the Conference of the Communist Party of Greater Budapest (an area comprising over 60% of Hungary's industry): " The Conference report says that productivity is stagnant in most industries and declining in some. Between February and July, it fell throughout the manufacturing industry by 17% . . . Far too many workers were applying for sick relief — in a recent week, in one factory : 11%. In another : 12%. Instances are given of self-inflicted wounds."

Referring to the decline in the quality of the goods produced, Rakosi also stated (August 31, 1949) that " waste in the Manfred Weiss iron foundry (Hungary's second largest factory) had risen from 10.4% to 23.5%."

On paper many workers still remained in the Party. Well, what would you do ? To leave would have meant the risk of being dubbed a ' fascist spy '. There was plenty of evidence of this. It made the incentive to stay in particularly attractive. Some proof of the crisis of conscience Party members were going through was shown by Jozsef Revai — the Party theoretician. In October 1948, he complained that *Szabad Nep*, the Party daily of which he was editor, was read by only 12% of Party members.

* * *

Meanwhile a few leading members of the Communist parties of Eastern Europe had become audacious. They had begun to think for themselves. Their thoughts were subversive of the established order. Party purges became popular.

Between 1948 and 1950, the Communist parties expelled : in Czechoslovakia over 250,000 members ; in Bulgaria 92,500 — about a fifth of the membership ; in Rumania : 192,000 — over a fifth of the membership. In Hungary, 483,000 Party members were expelled.

This was the period of the big Tito-Stalin explosion. The ' fallout ' contaminated Communist parties throughout the world. The sickness was, of course, most prevalent in Eastern Europe, where hunting Titoists became a fashionable sport for the various leaderships. Large numbers of people were arrested and thrown into prison. Show trials were held. Thousands of erstwhile ' good Stalinists ' were found guilty on clearly trumped-up charges. Many hundreds were executed. Among the leaders themselves, Slansky and Clementis in Czechoslovakia, Koci Xoxi in Albania, Kostov in Bulgaria, and Rajk in Hungary, all paid the supreme penalty. One of Kostov's most 'serious ' crimes was revealed by the Prosecution in dead-pan-comedian style. Kostov was charged with having

---

38. *Neue Zurcher Zeitung,* September 6, 1949.

been a friend of Bela Kun who, it had been ' proved ', was a ' Trotskyist fascist.'

The most truly frightening thing was Rajk's ' confession '. He was arrested in May, 1949, and his trial began on September 16. Rajk pleaded guilty to all the Prosecution's charges and to a number of others besides. That he could not possibly have been guilty of these charges, must have been quite obvious to those who knew him. Rajk and the others were sacrificed to bolster up the tottering authority of the Party leadership. These ' victorious ' Stalinists intended the trials to be shocking and frightening examples of their ruthlessness. They were. Through these judicial murders, Stalin, as chief spokesman for the bureaucracy, was saying to all: " Think twice before you question our infallibility." In Eastern Europe at this time, people might well have thought that Orwell's prophesy had been brought forward by several decades. But here again resistance was growing.

New Course?

> "... a stratum of the old state that had not cropped out but been upheaved to the surface of the new state by an earthquake; without faith in itself, without faith in the people, grumbling at those above, trembling before those below, egoistic towards both sides and conscious of its egoism, revolutionary in relation to the conservatives and conservative in relation to the revolutionists ..."
> K. Marx. *The Bourgeoisie and the Counter-Revolution* (1850).

On March 6, 1953, the Kremlin bluntly announced that Stalin had died after a short illness. Workers in Eastern Europe felt the time had now come to end the oppression his regime had imposed on them. They did not wait long. Early in June, workers in Plzen began a mass demonstration.

Plzen is one of Czechoslovakia's largest industrial centres. The great 'Skoda' arms factory is situated there. The demonstration, which was quite spontaneous, began as a protest against currency changes. But as it spread, political demands were made: greater participation in factory management, an end to piece-work, the resignation of the Government and free elections. By the time the demonstration had developed to the verge of a revolt (uniformed soldiers had joined in and large crowds had occupied the Town Hall), troops arrived from Prague and the rising was swiftly quelled. Further spontaneous risings in other parts of Czechoslovakia and in other satellite countries, were quickly crushed without reaching the world's headlines. Two weeks later, on June 17, 1953, the workers of East Berlin rebelled.

The revolt started with "a demonstration of building workers on the Stalin Allee.[39] Downing tools, they marched to the city centre to present their demands. ... Transport workers left their trams and lorries to join the demonstration. Factory workers rushed from their benches, students from the colleges, housewives from their homes and shopping, even schoolboys from their lessons. ... Soon, the revolt spread throughout Eastern Germany."[40]

The workers of East Berlin were not subdued until after they had waged bloody battles with Russian tanks. For several days, this revolt drew world wide attention, not only because it involved workers whose demands were political

---

39. Re-named "Karl Marx Allee." [November 14, 1961.]
40. Syndicalist Workers Federation pamphlet—*The Hungarian Workers' Revolution*, p.15.

as well as economic, but also because of Russia's direct and violent intervention. This intervention exposed the weakness of the Ulbricht regime.

After the Berlin uprising, the Kremlin adopted a 'new course'. Many reasons dictated this change of policy. The men in Moscow were certainly frightened by the Berlin events. Their lackeys in the capitals of Eastern Europe were shuddering as they felt the angry breath of the masses down their backs. They were all for 'changing course', but they knew that the Russian bureaucracy could grant them no major degree of autonomy, for it feared they might attempt to go the Tito way. The last thing Moscow wanted at this stage was to be seen using the tanks and bayonets of the Red Army to crush revolution throughout Eastern Europe.

* * *

A slight relaxation occurred in the U.S.S.R. itself. It was immediately reflected in the satellite countries.

In Hungary, early in July 1953, Malenkov himself 'advised' Rakosi to move into the background for a while. Imre Nagy, who had been Minister for Agriculture in the 1944 Government, Minister of the Interior in 1946, and had somehow survived the various purges, became Prime Minister. His first speech outlined the new programme.

In this first speech, Nagy criticised the revised plan of 1951 as too heavy a burden on the country. Greater consideration was to be given to light industry and to consumer goods. More material aid was to be given to collective and state farms, and also to individual peasant owners. A collective farm could be dissolved on a majority vote of its members. The special police tribunals were to be abolished. These were only concessions. But it is noteworthy that they were the most radical of all those made by the satellite leaderships during this period.

During the four months that followed Nagy's speech, a number of collective farms were dissolved—10% according to a speech that Rakosi (who remained Party Secretary) made to a plenary session of the Party's Central Committee on October 31. 1953. Rakosi also reported that some local officials were obstructing peasants who wished to leave the collectives. In a few cases, force had had to be used. Rakosi, who showed no real enthusiasm for the concessions, stressed that it was a Party decision that must be carried out by members. The Party, whether torturing and killing people or just throwing them a few crumbs, is always right.

The 'new course' was applied throughout 1954. The 'relaxation' was even noticeable to foreign visitors. In conversation, people were more ready openly to criticise the Government. Many political prisoners were released. There can be no doubt that Hungarians were breathing a little more freely.

When a smothered people begin to see daylight, when they

get the first whiff of fresh air, they tend to press strongly forwards. Their first ideas are to enlarge the holes, their second to tear down the whole throttling structure. This creates insoluble dilemmas for all ruling minorities—dilemmas felt the more acutely the more totalitarian their regimes.

*   *   *

All major decisions about Hungary were taken in Moscow. After Malenkov had 'resigned' and Krushchev had taken over, the Hungarians again sensed change in the air.

In real terms, Nagy's concessions had been small enough. But he was moving too quickly for the Kremlin. On April 18, 1955, the National Assembly decided, by a 'unanimous' vote, to relieve Nagy of his post. The Hungarians tensed when Rakosi was brought back to the centre of things. The feeble lights dimmed. The tragedy again reverted to macabre farce.

The long statement issued by the Central Committee showed some signs of the Party's discomfort. It accused Nagy of hindering the development of heavy industry and of collective farms, and of "using the Government machine as an instrument of repression against the Party." That Nagy was not immediately 'liquidated' reveals the uneasiness and indecision felt in the Kremlin about Hungary. 'Reconciliation' negotiations were proceeding between Tito and Krushchev.[41] Nagy was not called a 'Titoist' or a 'Fascist' when he was later expelled from the Party. He was simply labelled "an incorrigible, right-wing, deviationist".[42] To be called a 'deviationist' by Rakosi would stand a worse 'Stalinist'[43] than Nagy in good stead with the Hungarian people.

Most of the concessions granted over the twenty months of Nagy's rule were now subjected to 'salami tactics': they were slowly whittled away. The Secret Police, who for a while had remained discreetly in the background, now felt they could safely justify their high pay once again. Measures for the rapid development of collectivization were introduced. Pressure on workers for increased output was stepped up . . . to help fulfil Moscow's Five Year Plan[44]—a plan in which the Hungarian workers, incidentally, had never been consulted in any way.

In the Kremlin, the new leadership felt fairly secure. They had coped with the immediate repercussions of Stalin's death. The Plan seemed to be working. Leaders in the satellite

---

41. George Mikes says that Tito expressed dissatisfaction at the restoration of Rakosi. Krushchev replied: " I have to keep Rakosi in Hungary because, in Hungary, the whole structure will collapse if he goes."— George Mikes, *Hungarian Revolution*, p.61.
42. Peter Fryer—*Hungarian Tragedy.*
43. Nagy was a member of a Government and of the Party which had, for years, faithfully carried out all Stalin's wishes.
44. The first Hungarian Five Year Plan, which ended in 1954, was to be followed in 1955 by a second, " in close co-ordination with the Soviet Union." Other countries involved were Czechoslovakia, Rumania, Poland and East Germany.

countries boasted of increased outputs for 1955. In Hungary, industrial production was claimed to have increased by 8.2% over the figures for 1954. The methods used to extract this from reluctant workers hardly bear thinking of. The people had endured misery up till 1953—yet had shown they could resist. The relative clemency of the Nagy regime followed by the abrupt putting back of the clock to 1953 provoked a working class resistance greater than ever. Even harsher measures were needed to 'discipline' the masses.

But as far as the Kremlin was concerned, things seemed definitely on the mend. Khrushchev and his colleagues felt they had everything under control. This was an important consideration in their momentous decision to reveal that after all Stalin had not been God.

Poland Erupts

" The working class could not be the leading and most progressive section of the nation if reactionary forces were able to find support in its ranks. ' Agents provocateurs ' or reactionaries have never been the inspiration of the working class ; they are not and they never will be."
Gomulka. *Polish Facts and Figures* (November, 1, 1956).

At the 20th Congress of the Russian Communist Party, held in February 1956, Krushchev's ' revelations ' about Stalin caused a political earthquake. The foundations of every Communist party in the world were shaken. It will be decades before they are repaired—if ever they are. Were the ' revelations ' a ' tactical mistake ' ? Had the Russian bureaucrats not realized that, by de-godding God, the faithful might begin to question the whole theology proclaimed by his disciples ?

Did Krushchev know of the ferment growing in Poland and Hungary even before the 20th Congress ? Did he know that this was affecting the Polish Communist party itself ? Did he understand its potential danger both to his own regime and to those of his satellites ?

In Poland on the morning of June 28, 1956, the workers at the Zispo locomotive factory in Poznan struck. They walked out onto the streets. This was not done on impulse. Many weeks earlier a committee had been elected. It had presented the management with a list of demands. Some were predictable. They wanted pay increases, lower prices and lower piece-work norms. The management was startled, however, when these ' common workers ' criticised the way the factory was being run and demanded a different organization of work in the various shops. To question managerial infallibility in deciding what the workers were to do, and then to demand reorganization of shop floor production, struck at the very roots of the system. The managers did not go up through the roof. They did what their Western counterparts would have done : they adopted delaying tactics and called them ' negotiations '. These dragged on, without result. The workers eventually saw through them. In their thousands they took to the streets.

As the news spread, workers assembled in other plants. They voted to join the movement. The political character of the demonstrations then became apparent. Posters carried in the processions demanded such things as " Freedom and Bread ! ", "Out with the Russians ! " and " End Piecework ! "

Other people, taking their lead from the workers, joined in. As far as Poznan was concerned, the demonstrations soon showed the features of a full-scale uprising. Russian tanks and troops surrounded the city, but did not move in. The Government brought in Polish tanks whose crews did as they were told. Workers' blood flowed in the streets. After two days, the revolt was crushed. The Zispo factory management had their ' right ' to manage inscribed in blood. There were ' sympathetic ' strikes in several other towns, but they were quickly isolated by the police and did not reach similar proportions.

Shocked and confused, the Polish bureaucracy blamed the uprising on ' provocateurs ', on ' secret agents employed by the United States and Western Germany '. But on July 18, at a meeting of the Party's Central Committee, Edward Ochab, the First Secretary, said : " . . . it is necessary to look first of all for the social roots of these incidents (in Poznan) which have become, for the whole of our Party, a warning signal testifying to the existence of serious disturbance in the relations between the Party and various sections of the working class."

Ochab went on to explain that about 75% of the Poznan workers had suffered from a fall in wages, while the piece-work norms had increased. By giving only economic reasons for the uprising, Ochab was seeking to play down its important political aspects. His statement, nevertheless, appeared to reflect a more positive attitude to the workers' demands. It no doubt prevented further immediate uprisings in a nation still seething with discontent.

After Poznan, the demand for change increased. The badly shaken leadership tried to evolve a new policy—a ' Polish road to socialism '. Some anti-Stalinists were given posts in the Party. Gomulka, excommunicated and imprisoned in 1951, and under house arrest since 1954, was brought back into communion with the Party. He was issued a brand new membership card.

The attitude of the Polish leaders differed from that of the Communist hierarchy in the rest of Eastern Europe.[45] This worried the men in the Kremlin. So, while the Polish Communist Party's Central Committee was still in session, reviewing the Poznan events, the Russians sent their Premier, Marshal Bulganin, to Warsaw. He came to enforce the Russian line that Poznan was the work of " Western agents and provocateurs ". The Central Committee showed him they would not stand for outside interference. As soon as Bulganin arrived, the Central Committee meeting was suspended. After the formalities, it was politely suggested to

---

45. We do not have space here to describe the Russian treachery during the magnificent campaign of the Polish workers of Warsaw against the Nazis in 1944. This was a betrayal of such sickening magnitude that few Poles will ever forget it. The memory of these events played a large part in the post-war attitude of the Poles to the U.S.S.R.

Bulganin that he make a tour of the provinces. He agreed. The Central Committee then resumed its session. As soon as Bulganin returned to Warsaw, the Central Committee meeting was again suspended. The session was not resumed until he had finally left for Moscow. Bulganin's visit only succeeded in increasing anti-Russian feeling among the Polish people.

At the end of September, the first trials began. People were charged with ' anti-Socialist ' activity during the Poznan riots. The trials were less of a farce than those of pre-Poznan days. The defence was allowed some freedom. The sentences were relatively mild. In October 1956, the Government announced the postponement of further trials.

On October 19, another meeting of the Central Committee was convened, primarily to elect Gomulka Party leader. As the Committee met, it was reported that the Red Army in Poland had begun large-scale manoeuvres. Armoured units were moving towards Warsaw. While the Polish leaders were asking themselves whether this was some kind of threat, the answer walked in on them—Krushchev himself accompanied by a formidable detachment of the Kremlin 'Old Guard': Molotov, Mikoyan, Kaganovich and a smattering of generals. The news spread quickly. The workers formed groups and armed themselves. Their groups kept in close contact with the Polish Army.

Crisis point had been reached. The air was electric with the tension. Precise details of the clash between the Central Committee and the Krushchev circus are not yet known. But the main reason for the visit is known. Above all else, the Russians insisted that, in the elections that were about to take place, Marshal Rokossovski should retain his posts of Minister of Defence and Commander-in-Chief of the Polish Army. Gomulka refused and despite threats did not give way. He knew that in standing up to the Kremlin, he not only had a big majority of the people on his side: the workers, peasants and students. He also had a considerable proportion of the bureaucracy and of the Army behind him.

A war between Russia and Poland was the last thing the Kremlin wanted. The Russians did not insist. The Red Army was not called in. Krushchev knew that whatever Gomulka's attitude might now be, he would later be compelled to call on Russian help, both to maintain the Oder-Neisse frontier and to assist the Polish economy, which was in a chaotic condition. Within 24 hours, the Russians returned to Moscow. The following day, October 21, the Polish Politburo was elected. As expected, Gomulka became First Secretary of the Party. Changes in the Government, the Army and the Party were immediately initiated. Rokossovski resigned and returned to Moscow (where he was at once given the post of Russian Minister of Defence).

Gomulka had triumphed only in so far as he represented

the national aspirations of the Polish people. The base of his rule was still extremely narrow. He represented the interests of the Polish bureaucracy. Following the independent action taken by the Polish workers, and their insistent demands for a greater share in the management of their own affairs, the basis of the bureaucracy—even purged of its pro-Russian elements—remains both weak and unstable. An attempt to broaden the basis of the regime led Gomulka into an alliance with the ex-propertied class, through the Catholic Church. In exchange for a partial restoration of its former property and privileges, the Church threw its influence behind Gomulka. God and Gomulka were brought together through a joint fear of the working class. It is a temporary alliance —a mutual expedient. When the Polish workers take to managing their own affairs, they will put all these parasites right out of business.

Nearing Flashpoint

" **The time of surprise attacks, of revolutions carried through by small conscious minorities at the head of unconscious masses, is past.** Where it is a question of a complete transformation of the social organization, the masses themselves must also be in it, must themselves already have grasped what is at stake, what they are going in for, body and soul."
F. Engels. *Introduction to Marx's 'The Class Struggle in France'* (1895).

From the spring of 1956 on, the quick build-up of tension in Poland was paralleled by similar development in Hungary. The exposure of Stalin at the 20th Congress, in February 1956, gave further impetus to revolutionary tendencies in Hungary. These, already discernible in October 1955, now came more into the open.

In April, 1956, the 'Petöfi Circle '[46] was formed by the Young Communists—mainly students. Assisted by the Writers' Union. it soon became an important and effective centre for the dissemination of opinion, criticism and protest about the deplorable state of Hungarian society. Several other discussion groups were formed, but the Petöfi Circle remained the largest. (Similar discussions took place in Russia, prior to 1917.)

Many pamphlets were produced and distributed at this time, mainly in Budapest. A duplicating machine at Party Headquarters in Budapest is said to have been used. This could not have been done without the connivance of some members of the government. Due to shortages, there were production difficulties. It is reported that one pamphlet had been produced on toilet paper. In the early days, the main themes of this literature were purely demands for more literary freedom. But the political implications were clear. Later, the writers, all Communists, demanded that Hungary should follow her own road to Communism. They thereby clearly implied that the present road was wrong and that a greater independence from the U.S.S.R. was necessary.

Similar themes were now being discussed at the longer and longer meetings of the Petöfi Circle. The Rakosi government then banned these meetings. This made things worse.

---

46. Sandor Petöfi was a poet who played an important part in the Hungarian revolution against the Hapsburg oppression, in 1848. Czar Nicholas I sent troops to suppress the Hungarians.

The ban was soon lifted. The Communist writer, Gyula Hay[47] took the discussion a stage further. In an article in *Irodalmi Ujság* (Literary Gazette), he sharply attacked the bureaucratic interference with writers' freedom. Soon, the meetings of the Petöfi Circle were attracting thousands of people. These gatherings, already unanimous in their demands for intellectual liberty and truth, began to hear voices openly calling for political freedom.

One of these meetings was noteworthy for a passionate speech made by Mrs. Julia Rajk, widow of Laszlo Rajk, who had been executed as a " Titoist Fascist " in October, 1949. Several thousand people attended this meeting. It overflowed into the streets, where the speeches were relayed by loud-speakers. Mrs. Rajk called for justice to her husband's memory ; an honourable place in the Party's history. She severely criticised the off-hand way in which a few months earlier her husband had been " rehabilitated ". In a speech at Eger on March 27, 1956, Rakosi had casually announced that the Party had passed a resolution to rehabilitate Laszlo Rajk and others. This had been done officially, through the Supreme Court. In a cold voice, Rakosi had added that the entire Rajk trial had been based on a provocation. " It was a miscarriage of justice," he said. Julia Rajk then demanded that those guilty of his murder should be punished. This electrified the audience. Although there was no mention of Rakosi, everybody present knew exactly whom Julia Rajk meant.

By June, 1956, the intellectual agitation was in full swing. The articles in *Irodalmi Ujság* were becoming more and more bluntly critical of the regime. Although, earlier in the year, an issue of the paper had been confiscated, people were now quite surprised that the ' leadership ' did not suppress it. As the title suggests, the paper was primarily intended for people with literary interests. But many others were now reading it. Odd copies could be seen in the hands of factory workers, on the shop floor. In fact, demand for some issues so outstripped supply that a ' black market ' developed. Copies were selling at 60 forints—about 30s. each.

The articles by Gyula Hay suggested he was the centre of a campaign for freedom of the written word. During June this was sometimes referred to as the ' writers' revolt '. Officialdom reluctantly countenanced the situation. In fact, the June 28 issue of *Szabad Nep*[48] surprised many of its readers by welcoming this hitherto frowned-upon use of the human intellect. *Pravda* immediately countered the move.

---

47. Gyula Hay was well known at the time of Bela Kun's regime of 1919, when one of his plays was performed at the Hungarian National Theatre. He fled Hungary from Horthy's White Terror and wandered through Europe with a suitcase full of unperformed plays. He returned to Budapest at the end of World War II when another of his plays became a great success.

48. Communist Party daily.

It vehemently denounced the Hungarian writers. On June 30 the Central Committee brought *Szabad Nep* back to the Party line, with a resolution condemning the " demagogic behaviour " and " anti-party views " of " vacillating elements." It accused the writers of " attempting to spread confusion " with " the provocative content " of their articles. For once, part of the stereotyped party jargon was quite correct. This was indeed the precise intention of the revolutionary writers : to provoke thought, ideas and discussion about the existing conditions in Hungary. The Central Committee resolution was carried and hastily propagated at exactly the time when news of the workers' revolt in Poznan was reaching intellectual circles in Hungary and inspiring them to intensify their campaign.

The feeling of guilt among honest Communist intellectuals —members of long standing—became apparent. Their consciences no longer allowed the gulf between myth and reality to be bridged. At a large meeting of the Petöfi Circle on June 27, the novelist Tibor Dery had asked why they found themselves in such a crisis. " There is no freedom," he said. " I hope there will be no more Police terror. I am optimistic. I hope we shall be able to get rid of our present leaders. Let us bear in mind that we are allowed to discuss these things only with permission from above. They think it's a good idea to let some steam off an overheated boiler. We want deeds and we want the opportunity to speak freely."

In the first days of July, articles in *Irodalmi Ujság* began demanding Rakosi's resignation. The same demand was clearly voiced at the meetings of the Petöfi Circle. It was even suggested by some speakers that Imre Nagy should be brought back into the Party, although Nagy's name was only mentioned casually, even guardedly. Rakosi, who was in Moscow, returned suddenly to Budapest. He sought to suppress the heretical movement. He knew of only one way to do this : a purge. A list of prominent names among the politicians and writers was drawn up. But before the first stage (the arrests) could be carried out, Suslov, Russian Minister for the affairs of the People's Democracies, unexpectedly arrived in Budapest. He was immediately followed by Mikoyan. They told Rakosi that his plan would ignite an already explosive situation. The Kremlin had decided that Rakosi should go.

The smouldering crisis in Hungary was not the only reason for the Kremlin's decision. Tito hated Rakosi. He had for some time been agitating for his removal. Tito refused to meet Rakosi, or even to travel through the country where he held power. The Russo-Yugoslav rapprochement influenced the decision to get rid of Rakosi.

All this was clearly a Kremlin-inspired compromise. For Rakosi's close friend and collaborator, Ernö Gerö, was to succeed him as First Secretary. And, with the exception of General Farkas, who was expelled from the Party, most of Rakosi's followers retained their positions.

Hungarians heard of Rakosi's resignation on July 18. They also heard that the recently rehabilitated Janos Kadar and Gyorgy Marosan,[49] the Social Democrat, had been made members of the Political Bureau. These were the first of a few minor concessions made during the month of August. In the tumultuous situation, these concessions were to prove insignificant and wholly inadequate. The suffering of the working people had been too long and too great for them to harbour illusions about changes in the Leadership or to be bought off by a few extra coppers in their pay packets.

Through the long summer days the debate smouldered on. While the fireflies danced animatedly among the trees of the countryside, fascinating ideas about freedom flew about the meetings in the towns. Tension mixed strangely with a holiday mood. The whole month was like a heavy summer evening : the sun still glowing eerily through the dark purple clouds of a threatening storm. Familiar objects seemed out of perspective and took on a different shape and colour. In private rooms and public meeting places an ominous feeling of destiny pervaded the air. The intellectuals seemed to sense the ' dangers ' inherent in their ideas. Yet they felt compelled to carry on, on to whatever ends free expression might lead them to.

We have found no evidence throughout the whole of this restive period of any conscious attempt made by the intellectuals[50] to co-operate with the industrial workers on a mass scale, to share with them the experiences of this cultural and political awakening, and thus to demonstrate that the workers' struggles were bound up with the articulate demands for freedom, for truth, etc. Nevertheless, the Petöfi Circle had become, albeit not in a completely conscious manner, the articulate voice of the working people of Hungary. It may well be that, had such co-operation occurred, the Party leaders would have acted to suppress the movement sooner than they did. But they would have had to do so in the face of even greater solidarity than was to develop at the height of the revolution. In the event, the degree of co-operation, liaison and solidarity between workers and intellectuals was remarkably great. But closer co-operation with the workers earlier on would most certainly have broadened the base of the movement. The more practical and radical approach of the workers would have cleared the air of at least some of the cramping illusions held by many of the

---

49. Rakosi had kept them both in jail for years as " Titoist Fascists ", etc. Kadar still bore the marks on his face and body of the tortures he suffered on orders of the ' Leadership.'

50. We use the term loosely to describe the type taking part in this movement. There were, of course, a few industrial workers at the meetings, but the large majority were writers and students plus a number of schoolteachers, doctors, etc.

intellectuals—for example their great enthusiasm for a Nagy Government, appeals to Western leaders, to U.N.O., etc.

It was the veteran Communist writer, Gyula Hay, who again brought the cauldron to the boil with an article in the September 8 issue of *Irodalmi Ujság*. It poetically demanded " absolute and unfettered freedom " for writers.

The article stated that " it should be the writer's prerogative to tell the truth ; to criticise anybody and anything ; to be sad ; to be in love ; to think of death ; not to ponder whether light and shadow are in balance in his work ; to believe in the omnipotence of God ; to deny the existence of God ; to doubt the correctness of certain figures in the Five Year Plan; to think in a non-Marxist manner even if the thought thus born is not yet amongst the truths proclaimed to be of binding force ; to find the standard of life low even of people whose wages do not yet figure amongst those to be raised ; to believe unjust something that is still officially maintained to be just ; to dislike certain leaders ; to describe problems without concluding how they may be solved ; to consider ugly the New York Palais,[51] declared a historic building, despite the fact that millions have recently been spent on it ; to notice that the city is falling into ruins since there is no money to repair the buildings ; to criticise the way of life, the way of speaking and way of working of certain leaders ; . . . to like Sztalinvaros ; to dislike Sztalinvaros ; to write in an unusual style ; to oppose the Aristotelian dramaturgy ; . . . etc., etc. Who would deny that a short while ago many of those things were strictly forbidden and would have entailed punishment . . . but today, too, they are just tolerated and not really allowed."

About a week after Hay's article was published, the congress of the Writers' Union opened in Budapest. The depth of the revolt revealed itself in the elections for the new Presidium. All those who had supported the Rakosi regime, if only passively, were ousted. Communist ' rebels ' and some non-Communist writers were elected. All the speeches sharply criticised the " regime of tyranny." The rehabilitation of Nagy was demanded. Gyula Hay admitted that Communist writers, " having submitted to the spiritual leadership of the Party Secretariat, let themselves be led astray on to the path of mendacity." He added that the most honest writers had found themselves in a frightful dilemma and " suffered horribly in this atmosphere of lying . . . and paid dearly for the lie . . . with the lowering of the standard of our work.. . . ." Konya, the poet, took up the theme in an impassioned speech about writing only the truth. He ended with the rhetorical questions : " In the name of what morality do the Communists consider them-selves justified in committing arbitrary acts against their former allies, in staging witch-trials, in persecuting innocent

---

51. A famous coffee house damaged during the war and rebuilt by the Government.

people, in treating genuine revolutionaries as if they were traitors, in gaoling and killing them ? In the name of what morality ? "

Thus, the intellectuals exposed their crisis of conscience. Yet this resolute search for truth, amounting at times almost to mysticism, helped to give the events that followed an essential theme of socialist morality.

The First Demands

" Men make their own history, whatever its
outcome may be, in that each person follows
his own consciously desired end, and it is precisely the resultant of these many wills operating
in different directions and of their manifold
effects upon the outer world that constitutes
history. Thus it is also a question of what the
many individuals desire ".
F. Engels. *Ludwig Feuerbach and the End of
Classical German Philosophy* (1888).

Towards the end of September the first of the Poznan
trials began in Poland. Public sympathy with the accused
was apparent. Every possible opportunity was taken, both
by those on trial and the public, to condemn the violence
and injustice of the regime. The Government squirmed.
Almost all the accused were ordinary workers. The sentences were comparatively mild.

When this news reached the Hungarians they were elated.
The tension and the pressure on the Government increased.

The ruling group, feeling themselves more out of touch
than usual, tried to win sympathy with a stage-managed
funeral for Laszlo Rajk. Many of those who had stage-
managed his trial and execution as a " Titoist Fascist " now
indignantly deplored the " slander " of Comrade Rajk who
had been " innocently condemned and executed." Their
belief that they could deceive the people with such a macabre
exhibition proved their complete degeneracy. Over 200,000
people turned out for the funeral.[52] Even then the ' leaders '
did not see the light. They did not see that the demand
for Rajk's complete rehabilitation was purely symbolic. The
people had not forgotten the brutality of Rajk's secret police.
" One of the jokes current in Budapest at the time was: ' What
is the difference between a Christian and a Marxist ? The
Christian believes in a hereafter ; the Marxist believes in a
rehabilitation hereafter '."[53]

Rajk's exhumed corpse was re-buried on Martyrs' Day—
October 6. This was the anniversary of the execution by the
Austrians, on October 6, 1849, of the first constitutional Prime
Minister of Hungary, Count Batthány, and of thirteen others.
About three hundred young men discovered some connection
between this and the day's event. They began the first
unofficial demonstration. They marched to the Batthány

---

52. The *Daily Worker* carried no report of this very important event.
53. Peter Fryer—*Hungarian Tragedy*, p.39.

monument carrying posters and shouting slogans about independence and freedom. Several onlookers joined them believing that such a demonstration, however incredible, must have official sanction.

During September and early October the workers had become active. They were demanding ' genuine workers' self-government '[54] in the factories. The Trade Union Council, still controlled by the Party, gave these demands the universal ' leadership ' twist. It ' moderated ' them. The demands were revolutionary in the circumstances : broadening of trade union democracy ; establishment of workers' control ;[55] a prominent role for the unions in solving problems of production and management ; the manager to keep his " full right " to make decisions, but to consult the union committee on questions of wages and welfare. Here was the most important development in the whole of the campaign so far.

This remarkable political consciousness of the workers had its core in the concentrated industrial area of Czepel Island,[56] in the Danube between Buda and Pest. It immediately transformed the whole situation. Until now the campaign had been one of agitational ferment and protest. The workers' demand for ' self-government ' in the factories gave it a revolutionary edge in the strictest sense of the word. The workers were preparing for the psychological moment when their radical action would change the whole political and economic system. No wonder that, later on, the spokesmen of the West were to prove so uninformative !

The Petöfi Circle took up the workers' demands. But they were still unaware of their revolutionary implications. In a series of new demands, the Government was requested to hand over the administration of the factories to the workers. This must surely have appeared naïve to anyone aware of the nature of government. It tended to perpetuate the illusion that any government can act in the interests and on behalf of working people.

The Petöfi Circle also called for the expulsion of Rakosi from the Party ; for a public trial of General Farkas ; for a revision of the second Five Year Plan ; for equality in all relations between Hungary and the Soviet Union ; for full publication of all trade agreements (the trade pact with Moscow for the exploitation of the rich uranium deposits found a few months earlier at Pecs was stressed); and for the re-admittance of Nagy to the Party. A concession to the pressure came a few days later. Nagy was given a new Party card !

In mid-October, Gerö left to meet Tito in Belgrade. At

---

54. We call this 'workers' management'— see *Solidarity* pamphlet No. 6: *The Meaning of Socialism.*
55. Not necessarily a revolutionary demand. See *Solidarity* pamphlet No. 7—*The Workers' Opposition* p.66.
56. The great industrial area of Budapest renowned as ' Red Czepel ' because of the large number of its workers who were Party members.

precisely this time, momentous events were taking place in Poland. The Hungarian intellectuals were further inspired when they learned that the Kremlin and the old Polish leadership had been defeated, that Gomulka had been elected as First Secretary, that Rokossovski had resigned.

The Petöfi Circle called for a mass demonstration on October 23, " to express the deep sympathy and solidarity with our Polish brothers " in their struggle for freedom. They applied to the Ministry of the Interior for permission to hold the demonstration. It was granted ! All hell would have broken loose had it been refused.

By October 22, groups in the Hungarian universities and the various discussion circles were meeting. They considered the form of the demonstration. There was broad agreement that there should be a march to the statue of General Josef Bem, on the bank of the Danube. This seemed appropriate. Bem was a Pole who won fame when he fought with the Hungarians against the Hapsburg (Austrian) oppression in the so-called ' umbrella revolution ' of 1848-49. But there was some disagreement between two of the largest Budapest universities. The Central University wanted slogans and banners to make the purpose of the demonstration clear beyond doubt. The Polytechnic wanted a more ' aesthetic ' demonstration—no shouting, no banners, just a quiet march to the statue and back. A surprising development occurred at Szeged University, in Hungary's second largest city. A separate students' organisation, called MEFESZ, was formed. Many members of DISZ, the official Communist organisation, joined. The Party decided it was no use trying to oppose the re-grouping. To retain some influence, DISZ was instructed to welcome the new formation. Then DISZ went further. It decided to participate in the next day's demonstration.

By the end of October 1956, many years of misery, of being bullied and oppressed, manipulated and managed, had brought the Hungarian people to the brink of revolution. Yet the people were not fully aware of it. No plans had been laid, no conscious steps taken towards fundamental change. No leadership, in the generally accepted sense, had emerged. Nevertheless, the classical conditions for revolution were there. The build-up had occurred over a period of years. The culminating events were to be compressed into days—even hours.

The October 23 Demonstrations

> " Do not be afraid of the initiative and inde-
> pendence of the masses ; entrust yourselves to
> the revolutionary organisations of the masses."
> V. I. Lenin. *One of the Fundamental Questions
> of the Revolution* (1917).

In the absence of Gerö, now returning from Belgrade, the
Party was undecided about what should be done. Some,
believing they were expressing Gerö's wishes, wanted the
march banned. Others preferred the old tactic of infiltration
and take-over. Both views sprang from a degenerate and
bureaucratic attitude to events. Laszlo Piros, the Minister
of the Interior and a close associate of Gerö, had the final
word. On the morning of Tuesday, October 23, permission
to hold the march was withdrawn.

Delegations from the various groupings and universities
began to arrive at Party Headquarters in Academy Square.
A few were allowed in. They asked officials to use their
influence to get the ban withdrawn. Gyula Hay, and a small
delegation from the Petöfi Circle, argued for the lifting of
the ban. They explained that many students and writers
intended to march, permission or no permission. The
bureaucrats prevaricated.

By the afternoon, marchers were forming up in different
parts of the City. As is so often the case, rank-and-file
action caused a sudden change of mind at the Ministry of
the Interior. Deputy Minister Mihaly Fekete suddenly
announced on the radio that the ban had been lifted. The
'infiltration' faction had apparently won. Fekete patronis-
ingly added: " The employees and all the Communist Party
members of the Ministry of the Interior have rallied to the
side of honest Hungarians in the interests of change."

The demonstration was soon under way. Marchers were
converging on the Bem statue from numerous points in
Budapest. A crowd of several thousands had assembled at
the Petöfi statue and now joined the march. The Hungarian
national colours of red, white and green were much in
evidence. Improvised banners and posters appeared. Some
were simply inscribed " Freedom." Others added " Independence—Truth." Others still called for " Polish-Hungarian
Friendship." Among the many and diverse slogans, which

showed the individuality of the demonstrators, none was directly anti-Russian. Only one came anywhere near to it : " Let each nation keep its army to its own soil! "[57]

The various columns of marchers arrived at the Bem statue one after the other. They there fused into one great crowd. The large majority were young people. On the way their ranks had grown as people in the streets, women and children, had joined. A small number of workers left their jobs and tagged on, a little self-consciously. Even before all the marchers had arrived, spontaneous speeches were being made. The general theme was solidarity. Solidarity at home. International solidarity. Solidarity with the people of Poland was much stressed.

Considerable pathos was added when a student reminded the crowd of the 1849 revolution by reciting the words of Petöfi : —

> Our battalions have combined two nations
> And what nations ! Polish and Magyar !
> Is there any destiny that is stronger
> Than those two when they are united ?

When nearly 50,000 people had assembled, Peter Veres moved up to the foot of the statue to read a resolution from the Writers' Union. Its seven points can be summarised as follows :

"We want :

1. An independent national policy based on the principles of socialism.
2. Equality in relations with the U.S.S.R. and the People's Democracies.
3. A revision of economic agreements in the spirit of the equality of national rights.
4. The running of the factories by workers and specialists.
5. The right of peasants freely to decide their own fate.
6. The removal of the Rakosi clique, a post in the Government for Imre Nagy, and a resolute stand against all counter-revolutionary attempts and aspirations.
7. Complete political representation of the working class— free and secret ballot in elections to Parliament and to all autonomous organs of administration."[58]

As Peter Veres stepped down, the crowd applauded. They had listened in almost total silence. Indeed, why should they have become particularly excited ? In some respects, the resolution was remarkably vague. There was really very

---

57. Perhaps this was carried by the student who, at the Polytechnic the previous evening, had caused an apprehensive hush to fall on the meeting when he suddenly shouted: " Out with the Russians!" There was some laughter when the silence was broken by the quiet voice of a lecturer: " Our friend means, of course, to suggest that it would be desirable for each nation to keep its army on its own soil."

58. For the full text of the resolution, see Appendix I.

little in it that Krushchev himself had not advocated at some time or other. The demands could, it is true, have been developed into a revolutionary programme. No mention was made of how all this might be achieved, even as it stood.

The demonstration was over. The crowds began to move away, but not to disperse. For some unknown reason they marched towards Parliament Square. Another crowd of several thousands joined them on the way. When they reached the Square they just stood there, in silence. People were now converging on Parliament Square in their hundreds. Many of the later arrivals had heard Gerö make his expected speech on the radio. Snatches from the speech were passed on, in low, angry voices. Faces at the windows of the Parliament building stared out at the crowd, which must now have numbered about a hundred thousand. Perhaps those at the windows became afraid. Suddenly all the lights in the building and in the square went out. The crowd remained where it was. Someone struck a match and lit a newspaper. Newspapers flared up all over the square. The people watched the building take on a gaunt, menacing look in the flickering yellow light. Perhaps they were thinking of what Gerö had just said : the students' demonstration had been an attempt to destroy democracy . . . to undermine the power of the working class . . . to loosen the friendly ties between Hungary and the Soviet Union . . . whoever attacks our achievements will be repelled . . . the intellectuals had heaped slanders on the Soviet Union ; they had asserted that Hungary was trading with the Soviet Union on an unequal footing, that independence must allegedly be defended, not against the imperialists, but against the Soviet Union. All this was an impudent lie — hostile propaganda which did not contain a grain of truth. After more such accusations, Gerö had said that the Central Committee would not meet for eight days.

Was this why the people now stood silently in Parliament Square ? Or were they just dumbfounded and exasperated by Gerö's intransigent stupidity? Was it really possible that hypocrisy could be taken so far ? The sheer mendacity left one speechless. Why deny so vehemently what everybody knew to be fact ?

A discussion began in one corner of the Square. After a while, voices from the darkness suggested that a delegation should go to the Radio station, in Sándor Street, with the request that their demands be broadcast. There were cries of agreement from the crowd. Then more discussion. Eventually a deputation moved off in the direction of Sándor Street . . . followed by 100,000 people! They now wanted to see *some* action, if only a broadcast, result from their silent vigil in Parliament Square. As this mass of people moved through the streets, they were joined by several thousand more, many of them industrial workers on their way home.

Further along the road, a group in the crowd decided to visit the City Park where stood a 26 foot, bronze statue of Stalin, the ' Man of Steel '. Two or three thousand people peeled off from the body of marchers and joined them. They were in great spirits, singing and laughing. When they reached the statue, a ladder and a tough rope were passed up onto the massive plinth. The ladder was put against the pedestal. Up climbed two men. A rope was placed around ' Stalin's ' neck. It was grabbed by hundreds of eager hands. It tautened. The statue grated and creaked as it bowed, slowly, to the crowd. With a final screech, it fell from its pedestal. There was an ear-splitting clang as it hit the plinth. A great cheer was followed by a roar of hilarious laughter. The whole thing was ludicrous. It was absurd. The plinth now looked even more grotesque. Still firmly planted on the pedestal were ' Stalin's ' 6-foot-high jack-boots. The rest of the statue was taken away by lorry and dumped in front of the National Theatre, where a laughing crowd soon smashed it to pieces.

Stalin's boots, however, still stood there. What an omen for those who believed in such things! It is not much use getting rid of one man. Another will always fill his boots. You must get rid of the need for rulers. Perhaps somebody thought about this, for later a Hungarian flag appeared in one of the boots. This red, white and green tricolour, with the Communist hammer and wheatsheaf emblem raggedly cut from its centre, was the only symbol of revolution the people knew.

The main crowd marching from Parliament Square had in the meantime arrived at the entrance to Sándor Street. It had been joined by many thousands more, mostly workers. Many had rushed there from all over Budapest. They had heard Gerö's speech (which had been broadcast at 6 p.m. and again at 7). The spontaneous decision of the demonstrators to go to the Radio Station particularly appealed to the workers. Traffic in the centre of the city had come to a standstill. The municipal police, though somewhat perplexed, made no attempt to interfere with the ' unofficial ' marchers. But the entrance to Sándor Street was barred by a shoulder-to-shoulder line of the dreaded A.V.O. men. They had also occupied the Radio Building. A machine-gun-carrying detachment stood on guard outside. The marchers stopped. There had obviously been members of the A.V.O. among the crowd in Parliament Square. On hearing the intention of the crowd to march to the Radio Station, they had informed their leaders.

The demonstrators craned their necks to see why the march had halted. They saw the glint of arms held by the grim-faced Security Police. Although unarmed, they no longer felt fear. In their solidarity, they recognised their strength. They glimpsed the possibility of freedom. Their destiny was in their hands alone. Yet none advocated violence against their oppressors.

" Let us pass! "—" The Hungarian people must hear our proposals! "—" Send in a delegation! ". These demands were shouted from various points in the crowd. Each demand was greeted with great applause. There was some discussion among the front ranks. A delegation was formed. After a further discussion with the A.V.O., this small group of people was let through the cordon and then into the Radio Building.

The crowd waited. The air rumbled with conversations. Occasional laughter was heard, even the snatch of a song. They were still in good mood. An hour passed. No sign of the delegation. The crowd's gaiety gave way to more serious determination. Some people were growing restless. The front ranks were now touching the A.V.O. cordon. Another half-hour. Still no word from their comrades in the building. The mood changed rapidly. Angry shouts flew up from all parts of the crowd. The armed cordon began to bulge a little. The A.V.O. men were clearly worried. After all, according to official rules and regulations, the people shouldn't really be there at all. And there were so many of them! People across the whole width of the road. People as far as the eye could see!

" Where's our delegation ? "—" Let them out! "—" Free our delegates! "— roared the crowd impatiently. A spontaneous surge forward swept the A.V.O. cordon aside. The people halted in front of another line of A.V.O. men guarding the Radio Building. Policemen throughout the world are not noted for either intelligence or understanding. The Hungarian Security Police were no exception. What should they do ? The demonstrators were unarmed — but there were thousands of them and they were angry. In any case, demonstrations of this sort were illegal. For their protection, ruling minorities always staff their police forces with men whose minds only work one way. The A.V.O. men knew only one answer. Machine-guns fired.

Agonized shrieks arose as the front ranks of the peaceful demonstrators crumpled to the ground. The crowd became infuriated. The police were quickly overwhelmed, their arms used to fire at the windows of the Radio Building from which lead now streaked into the throngs below.

The Hungarian Revolution had begun.

Nagy Calls in Russian Tanks

"The Party fights for a more democratic Workers and Peasants Republic, wherein the police and the standing army would be completely eliminated and replaced by a general arming of the people, by a universal militia ; all the offices would be not only elective but also subject to instant recall by a majority of electors ; all offices without exception would be paid at the rate of the average wage of a skilled worker ; all representative parliamentary institutions would gradually give place to Soviets . . . functioning both as legislative and executive bodies."
V. I. Lenin. *Materials relating to the Revision of the Party Programme* (May 1917).

The news spread fast. Within half an hour of the first shots in Sándor Street (and while Radio Budapest was continually broadcasting messages to the effect that " armed fascist and counter-revolutionary bands were attacking public buildings in the city ") the truth about the events at the Radio Building was known by almost everyone in town. The rest of the country knew soon after.

During the months of intellectual ferment, little had been heard of workers' opinions. On October 21, a worker from a factory in Czepel had said: " Rest assured, we too shall speak."[59] Now the workers spoke with deeds. Those who had earlier left the arms factories returned there. Their comrades of the night shift helped load lorries with commandeered arms : revolvers, rifles, light machine guns and ammunition. Many on the night-shift then left the factories and went to Sándor Street to help distribute the weapons and join the ever-increasing crowds. The police made no attempt to disperse the demonstrators. Many handed over their weapons to the workers and students, then stood aside ; some policemen joined the demonstration. This also applied to the soldiers. Large numbers of soldiers handed over their arms. Although the majority did not fight alongside the revolutionaries, practically none fought against them. This is easily explained. The majority of soldiers were young

---

59. Quoted from *Socialisme ou Barbarie*—vol. IV, No. 20, p.87.

peasants. The peasants had been less affected by the general ferment.

While fighting continued in Sándor Street and efforts were being made to occupy the Radio Station, thousands of workers and students began to form groups in the surrounding streets. These groups spread out into the city. They set up road controls and occupied some of the main squares. All cars were stopped. If members of the A.V.O. were found inside, the car was commandeered and the occupants sent off on foot. There was no general attack on the A.V.O. at this stage.

By 1 a.m., all the main streets and squares (including Parliament Square) had been 'occupied' by vast crowds. Large groups carrying an assortment of small arms stationed themselves at vantage points.

Gerö's lies were still coming from the radio ; over the incongruous signature of the Council of Ministers of the Hungarian Peoples Republic. "Fascists and reactionary elements have launched an armed attack on our public buildings and on our security units. To restore order, and until further measures are taken, all meetings, gatherings and marches are banned. The armed security organs have been ordered to apply the full vigour of the law against anyone who breaks this order." Later in the night, the term 'Fascists' was altered to 'counter-revolutionaries.' Of course, no mention was made of the machine-gunning by the A.V.O., nor of the killing of many of the unarmed people taking part in a peaceful demonstration.

It must be emphasized that although the situation had now reached the proportions of an armed uprising, *it had not in any way been planned or organized.* Many commentators throughout the world either claimed the whole thing had been previously organised or simply failed to mention its spontaneity. Whether their allegiance was to East or West, they were unable to understand that ordinary people could take effective action against the State without hierarchical and top-heavy organisation.

As we have previously shown, both the Russian rulers and the Western Powers had kept many Nazi administrators in position after the war. A hierarchical organisation, based on privilege, and reinforced by a rigid chain of command from above down, was for them the very essence of 'efficiency'. Their minds had been conditioned to see this structure as the only one possible. Understandably, but wrongly, they believed that the efficiency of the Hungarian revolutionaries must depend on some form of organisation similar to their own. How else, they argued, could ordinary workers, students and others have had such an excellent system of communication ? How else could they have armed themselves with such speed and smoothness ? The events in Hungary during the last week of October 1956 show clearly that the workers relied on quite different methods of organisation. If revolutionaries organise like those whose rule they seek to overthrow, they are defeated before the battle is engaged.

* * *

During the early hours of Wednesday October 24, workers and students were dying in the streets for the ultimate freedom to decide how to run their society. The Party leaders meanwhile were engaged in various manoeuvres. Gerö arranged for the Premier to be relieved of his post. Andras Hegedüs, an obedient stooge of Rakosi, had been little heard of even before he had been made Prime Minister. Now he was out. Gerö invited Nagy to take over. There is no evidence that Nagy needed any persuasion or that he made any conditions. No official announcement was made of this re-shuffle. The first the people knew of it was when, at 7.30 that morning, the radio referred to Nagy as the "Chairman of the Council of Ministers"—the official term for Prime Minister.

At 7.45 a.m. the radio announced that the Minister of the Interior had proclaimed martial law " as mopping-up operations against counter-revolutionary groups engaged in looting[60] are still in progress ". At 8 a.m. came the shocking announcement that, under the terms of the Warsaw Treaty, the Government had asked for help from Russian military units stationed in Hungary—" The Soviet formations, in compliance with the Government's request, are taking part in the restoration of order."[61]

There is no doubt that Imre Nagy was Prime Minister of the Government which called in Russian troops. There is some doubt about whether he was tricked into doing so. A large number of students and intellectuals felt Nagy had ' betrayed ' them. Their esteem for him dropped. At a crucial stage in the struggle, their morale took a severe jolt. But why should so many intellectuals have had illusions about Nagy ? Nagy was concerned with ' order '. He had never shown that his idea of ' order ' was any more than a liberalised form of the ' order ' that had prevailed in satellite Hungary. And in the situation prevailing on October 24, 1956, any demand for *this* kind of order had long ago been eclipsed by the people's desire and all-out struggle for far more fundamental change. A man of Nagy's background was bound to believe, like Gerö, that the massive force of Russian tanks would soon restore ' order '. He had been in the first Russian puppet government. He had, in turn, been Minister of Agriculture, Minister of the Interior, Mini-

---

60. It is remarkable that, during the whole course of the revolution. no cases of looting were reported by any observers other than die-hard Stalinists.
61. Hubert Ripka, *Eastern Europe in the Post War World*, p.163.

ster of Food, Minister of Agricultural Deliveries, and Deputy Prime Minister. He knew the ropes and where power lay. One of the main reasons for the naivety of the intellectuals was their lack of contact with industrial workers. There was, to some extent, a mutual embarrassment and suspicion. But action, the revolt itself, had brought them together as nothing else could have done. It was the workers who, on the morning of Wednesday, October 24, saved the struggle from complete collapse. They saw the Nagy issue as largely irrelevant. In the society they were glimpsing through the dust and smoke of the battle in the streets, there would be no Prime Minister, no government of professional politicians, and no officials or bosses ordering them about. The decision to call in Russian troops only strengthened the morale and resolve of the workers. They were now more determined than ever to fight to the end, whatever that end might be.

* * *

Thousands had spent the early hours of Wednesday in the streets or at meetings. A revolutionary council of workers and students was formed in Budapest and remained in permanent session. Radio Budapest continued to pour out lies : " The revolt is about to collapse ; thousands have surrendered to the authorities ; those who don't surrender will be severely punished ; no action will be taken against those who surrender." " Fascists, misguided patriots, counter-revolutionaries, bourgeois, bandits ". Persuasion, threats, cajoling, ranting. The purpose of propaganda is not to convince, but to confuse. It failed as far as the Hungarians were concerned. They knew it was all lies.

In Sándor Street, the Radio Building was repeatedly and furiously attacked. Later, the ' boys ' (one of the names Hungarians affectionately gave to the fighters) succeeded in occupying it. But the transmitters remained in the hands of the A.V.O. who concentrated all their effort in holding them. Heading the small group of announcers who kept the station operating was one György Szepesi, a sports commentator. During the first days of November, a group of workers searched the whole of Budapest for Szepesi, but he had disappeared.

The Battle is Joined

"A revolution is certainly the most authoritarian thing there is. It is the act whereby one part of the population imposes its will upon the other part by means of rifles, bayonets and cannons — authoritarian means, if such there were . . ."
F. Engels. *On Authority* (1872).

By 8.30 a.m., reports were circulating in Budapest that workers had already been involved in battles with Russian tanks on the outskirts of the city. Another report, less widely circulated, was that Suslov and Mikoyan had arrived in Budapest at dawn. They had apparently flown direct from Moscow, where the Kremlin was getting worried at the mess their men in Budapest were making of things. Mikoyan, it was alleged, had become very angry with Gerö. Whether this was true or not, it soon became known that Gerö had been 'relieved of his post' as First Secretary of the Communist Party. Janos Kadar was given the job. Many among the Communist hierarchy thought this a master move. Kadar was of working-class origin. He had spent a long time in prison as a Titoist. He had suffered considerably. He had been tortured—missing fingernails and scars on various parts of his body were proof of this. It is said he was a frightened man—frightened of pain. Understandably so. He was to prove soft clay in the hands of a ruthless 'leadership'!

Just after 9 a.m., Nagy broadcast a personal appeal as Prime Minister. He called for an end to the fighting. He asked that order be restored.

"People of Budapest! I announce that all those who, in the interest of avoiding further bloodshed, stop fighting before 1300 hours today and lay down their arms, will be exempted from summary jurisdiction. We shall realise as soon as possible, by all means at our disposal and on the basis of the June 1953 Government Programme, as I expounded it at that time in Parliament, the systematic democratisation of the country in every sphere of Party, State, political and economic life. Every possibility exists for the Government to realise my political programme by relying on the Hungarian people, under the leadership of the Communists. Heed our appeal. Cease fighting and secure the restoration of calm and order in the interest of the future of our people and country. Return to peaceful and creative work."

Does this sound like the speech of a man incapable of

calling in Russian troops ? First, the implied threat, clothed as a concession : " If you stop fighting by 1 p.m., you'll only be subject to normal (?) legal proceedings. If you don't then summary jurisdiction." All knew what summary jurisdiction meant. And what about " laying down arms " ? This meant surrendering their newly acquired weapons to the authorities.

Why should Nagy have hoped that workers fighting Russian tanks, the A.V.O. and the whole rotten bureaucratic set-up, should suddenly hand in their arms that Wednesday morning? At that very time, the workers and students had every reason, on the contrary, to intensify their struggle. And what of " the June 1953 Government Programme " ? Such a programme had been made redundant by the events of the last few days. It might have worked in April. On October 24, it appeared ridiculous. It may be true that Nagy was the most humane and liberal in the Hungarian Communist hierarchy. But he was a prisoner of certain ideas which clashed with the people's desire for fundamental political and economic change. It was beyond Nagy's comprehension to grasp what the people really wanted—what they were now striving towards.

Even if we accept that Nagy was honest and sincere, he must have shown an incredible naivety to talk, at *this* stage, of " the Hungarian people under the leadership of the Communists ". Leadership ? This was precisely what the people were against. This seemingly negative approach implied a very positive one : to make and carry out *their own* decisions. The only effect of Premier Nagy's first speech was to strengthen the resolve of most revolutionaries to fight on. As we shall see later, the people had already begun to build their own revolutionary organisations. As early as the first morning of the armed struggle. leaflets were being distributed in Budapest calling for a general strike. The imprint on these leaflets was : " The Revolutionary Council of Workers and Students."

* * *

Russian tanks had begun to enter the city at various points during the morning of October 24. Some units were immediately attacked by workers and students. Others were attacked after they had taken up strategic positions and opened fire. In some places, neither side opened fire. Here, students who had learnt Russian at school, were in conversation with the soldiers. It was explained that they were ordinary Hungarians—workers. A number of the young Russian soldiers seemed quite embarrassed. Perhaps they remembered some of the things they had been taught at school. Perhaps parts of ' Marxism-Leninism ' did not quite accord with what was now required of them.

Increasingly bitter battles were now raging throughout Budapest : at Baross Square outside the Eastern Railway Station, by the Ferencvaros railway freight station, around the Party Buildings of the 13th District, and in the streets around the statue of General Bem, scene of the peaceful demonstrations of the previous afternoon. Tanks of the 'Union of Soviet Socialist Republics', 'workers' tanks', were firing 'workers' shells'. The bodies of Hungarian workers were being torn to pieces.

Two of the biggest battles were at Széna Square and at the Killian Barracks. At Széna Square, in Buda, many thousands of people waited not knowing exactly what to expect or what to do. The majority were industrial workers ; but there were also many students, some of them young women. This was the general social composition of the revolutionaries. There were also schoolboys and even some schoolgirls. Most of them were armed.

The main idea was to stop all cars and see who was in them. They had found that by using hundreds of barrels to barricade the middle of the roads leading into the square, they could do this with ease. There were several gunfights with the occupants of cars who opened fire as soon as they saw the barrel barricade and its armed defenders. Several people were killed and wounded. Later the barricades were strengthened when workers brought onto the streets railway coaches and wagons from a nearby goods yard. Although some wagons were loaded with goods, nothing was taken at any time—a further indication of the people's awareness of the nature of their revolution.

Soon, all entrances to the Square were barricaded. The throb of powerful engines was heard and the first Russian tank rumbled into sight. It picked a weak spot in the barricade and went right through the centre of the Square. It was only attacked with a few odd rifle shots. Workers rushed to repair the breach. Then came two more tanks and two armoured cars. There was a heavy burst of machine gun and rifle fire from the revolutionaries. The first tank swung round and retreated down the road. The second rammed the barricade and, pushing a wagon along in front of it, moved slowly across the Square. Although attacked with Molotov cocktails, it rumbled on. The armoured cars were put out of action. All eight occupants were killed.

It had now become clear that the barricades had not been built to the best advantage. They were again strengthened. This time, the toughest obstacles were concentrated in the centre of the road, thus forcing the tanks to pass near to or on the pavements. Molotov cocktails could then be dropped on to them with far greater success from the windows of buildings lining the road.

A 'Molotov cocktail' is a home-made petrol bomb. It can be a very effective weapon, even against heavy armour. The Hungarians found them easy to make and fairly easy to use. Screw-top beer or lemonade bottles were used. The bottles were filled with petrol and the top very tightly screwed on. If non-screw-top bottles were used, it was imperative for them to be very securely sealed. A piece of dry rag (which was sometimes soaked in methylated spirit) was then firmly attached to the bottle by a wire around a ridge in its neck, or by strong elastic bands. Before throwing, the rag was lit. As the bottles hit the Russian tanks the glass would break and the petrol would ignite, often with devastating effect.

*   *   *

As the battle progressed, the workers and students in Szena Square improved their fighting methods. They were quite undisciplined in the military sense. There was no saluting, no bawling of orders. In their motley dress, their small arms looking like toys against the thick armour and big cannons of the tanks, they no doubt appeared pathetic to the 'orderly' military mind. But before Saturday, these few thousands of undisciplined workers and students had put some thirty Russian tanks out of action. They were a true vanguard of the working class. They fought with great courage, ardour, initiative and even humour. When a Russian tank caught fire, their cheers echoed from the buildings around the square. When a tank retreated, the Square was filled with cheers and laughter.

It was the same in the streets around the Killian Barracks. A group of workers had got hold of a small field gun which they operated from the front of the Corvin Cinema, on the Boulevard. The cinema, Budapest's largest, stood back from the other buildings in the street to form a 'bay'. When under extra-heavy fire, the gun was run back into the shelter of this bay. A tram conductor was put in charge of the aiming and firing of the gun. He and the others sometimes pulled their artillery up the street, to the Barracks at the junction of Ulloi Road and the Boulevard. From there they could shell targets in Ulloi Road until forced back to the Corvin Cinema. During lulls in the fighting, the gun crew would sit smoking and talking shop—revolution was their business. " At one time the discussion became so absorbing that a couple of Russian tanks had got into the Boulevard and were getting perilously close to the Cinema. There was a concerted rush to man the gun. Some way behind them came an odd figure in a furious shuffle to get to the gun. Under his arm was a crumpled newspaper, his hands sought frantically to pull his trousers up from around his ankles. ' Caught with your trousers down, eh ? ' came the inevitable jibe. The laughter continued as they made the gun ready. They fired the first round almost at point-blank range. It hit the first tank which exploded. The second tank immediately turned and retreated, but was caught in a crescendo of cross fire at the road junction. It stopped dead. Firing ceased. Thousands of eyes watched the tank. Suddenly, the Russian crew clambered out with their hands held high. A group of workers escorted them to the Killian Barracks."[62]

---

62. Related by Matyas Bajor—see Appendix IV.

The Barracks had been taken over by a Hungarian army unit led by Colonel Pál Maléter, which had sided with the people. Maléter's men were supported by a large number of workers and students. Once inside the Barracks, the civilians armed themselves. Throughout the Thursday they were under heavy fire from Russian guns. Towards evening three Hungarian tanks appeared on the scene and took up strategic positions near the Barracks. They went into action the next morning. Each day and all day, the battle raged around the Killian Barracks and in the adjoining side streets. At night, things were relatively quiet, for the Russian tanks always withdrew.

For nearly three days the struggle in Budapest had continued relentlessly. On Friday the Russians brought in four big field guns to pound the Killian Barracks into submission. Pál Maléter and the soldiers and civilians occupying the barracks had no heavy weapons other than their faith in themselves and in what they were doing. They fought. The workers in the streets fought. The tram conductor and his ' boys ' at the Corvin Cinema fought . . . with their one small gun. Through determination, courage and a flair for doing the unexpected, they not only kept the Russian gun crews on their toes, but caused them first drastically to restrict their fire and within two hours all four guns had been rendered useless.

Throughout the fighting, Radio Budapest alternated between calls to the freedom fighters (involved in this, that or the other big battle) to surrender, and reports that one or other group of freedom fighters had or was about to capitulate. This incredible radio station was now listened to strictly for laughs.

The Massacres

"Working men's Paris, with its Commune, will be forever celebrated as the glorious harbinger of a new society. Its martyrs are enshrined in the great heart of the working class. Its exterminators history has already nailed to that eternal pillory from which all the prayers of their priests will not avail to redeem them."
K. Marx. *The Civil War in France* (1871).

At a meeting of students and workers in Magyaróvár on Wednesday, October 24, it was decided to send a delegation the following morning to A.V.O. headquarters to ask them to remove the Soviet star from the front of the building. Soon after 10 a.m. on the 25th a large crowd of students and workers, including many women and children, met in the park. About two thousand people then began to march to the A.V.O. buildings. They were unarmed. The demonstration had been openly planned, and the A.V.O. had been busy during the night digging two trenches in front of their headquarters. Each trench now held two machine guns, manned by A.V.O. officers. The crowd stopped. Four workers walked the hundred yards or so and spoke to these officers. "We request you not to shoot. We are peaceful demonstrators." "All right," said one of the officers, "come nearer!" The crowd moved forward. All the machine guns then opened fire. Many people crumpled to the ground. At first, people at the back didn't believe they were being fired at. Then, starting from the front rows, from where the bloody corpses could be seen,[63] people began throwing themselves to the ground. From the roofs of the buildings, A.V.O. men began throwing grenades into the crowd. 101 people were killed and over 150 seriously wounded, including women and children.

When this dreadful news reached Györ, a little later, a large number of 'freedom fighters' set out in lorries for Magyaróvár. They arrived in the afternoon and joined the now-armed battalions of workers and students of Magyaróvár and of the neighbouring town of Moson. The A.V.O. barracks were surrounded. The people wanted the gun crews. They got them. Some were just beaten to death. Others were hanged upside down, beaten to death and their bodies slashed. This was done by a grim, silent crowd.

---

63. All observers interviewed say dum-dum bullets were used.

In Budapest on the 25th, an unarmed crowd had begun to march slowly to the Parliament Square from Rákócziút. They carried national flags with the 'communist' emblem torn from the centre. They also bore black flags in honour of those killed. According to Charles Coutts[64], they met a Russian tank on the way : "The tank stopped. A soldier put his head out and the people in the front of the crowd began to explain they were unarmed and were engaged in a peaceful demonstration. The soldier told them to jump on the tank : a number of them did so, and the tank set off in the demonstration. I have a photograph of this.

"Entering Parliament Square they met another Soviet tank which had been sent to fire on them. This tank, too, turned and joined the demonstration. In the Square were three more Soviet tanks and two armoured cars. The crowd went right up to them and began to talk to the soldiers. The Soviet commandant was saying : 'I have a wife and children waiting for me in the Soviet Union. I don't want to stay in Hungary at all', when suddenly from the roof tops there were three salvoes of gun-fire. Some of the people ran to the sides of the Square for shelter. Others were told by the Russians to shelter behind their tanks. Some thirty people, including a Soviet officer, were left lying on the Square either dead or wounded."[65]

Who fired from the roofs ? Coutts thought it was the A.V.O. Who else could it have been ? Their reason was obvious—to provoke the fraternising Russians into action, to harden their seeming softness. The friendship of the insurgents towards the Russian soldiers who refused to shoot them was later shown in a resolution of the Budapest Revolutionary Council which demanded "that they be accorded right of asylum in Hungary."

---

64. A British Communist who had lived in Budapest for three years. Editor of *World Youth*.
65. Related by Peter Fryer in *Hungarian Tragedy*, p.46.

The Workers' Councils

> " Those miners were not concerned with the
> question as to whether or not they should have
> a President. They seized the mine, and the
> important question to them was how to keep the
> cables intact so that production might not be
> interrupted. Then came the question of bread,
> of which there was a scarcity. All the miners
> again agreed on the method of obtaining it.
> Now this is a real programme of the revolution,
> not derived from books. This is a real seizure
> of power, locally."
> V. I. Lenin. *The All-Russian April Conference
> of the Russian Social Democratic Labour Party*
> (May 1917).

In the thick of the fighting on Thursday 25, Nagy came
again to the microphone of Budapest Radio.

" As Chairman of the Council of Ministers, I hereby
announce that the Hungarian Government is initiating
negotiations on relations between the Hungarian People's
Republic and the Soviet Union, concerning among other
things, the withdrawal of Soviet forces stationed in Hungary.
. . . I am convinced that Hungarian-Soviet relations built on
that basis will provide a firm foundation for a sincere and
true friendship between our peoples." Meanwhile, the
struggle in the streets of Budapest went on more fiercely
than ever. As it developed, so did the strike.

The strike began on the morning of Wednesday 24. It
spread quickly through the industrial suburbs of Budapest—
Czepel, Rada Utca, Ganz, Lunz, Red Star—then out into
the industrial centres of the country—Miskolc, Györ, Szolnok, Pecs, Debrecen. In Budapest, almost the whole population had risen. In the industrial areas, the revolution was
carried out exclusively by workers. Everywhere the workers
formed 'councils': in the factories, in the steel mills, in
the power stations, in the coal mines, in the railway depots.
Everywhere they thrashed out their programmes and demands.
Everywhere they armed themselves. In a number of places
they fought. Hubert Ripka[66] comments that, in the middle
of the fighting, workers proclaimed " a programme of radical
and political social change. This was a spontaneous develop-

---

66. Hubert Ripka was a minister in the post-war government of Czechoslovakia, during the presidency of Benes. After the Communist coup
of 1948, he went into exile. He died in 1958. Ripka was certainly not
a revolutionary socialist. Just as certainly, he was no fascist. He was
one of the more liberal-minded Czech social democrats.

ment. There were no governmental directives or any central leadership . . . Workers' Councils took over the management of the factories. . . In Hungary they were born of a spontaneous popular movement, and they soon became the living organs of a rising democracy and the effective instruments of a fighting revolution."[67]

Radio Budapest's news broadcasts referred to the strike and to the formation of workers' councils as " industrial disturbances ". " Public demonstrations " in the towns and cities of the various industrial regions, were constantly referred to. There were also repeated announcements that, in such-and-such a city, " calm " had returned and that workers should therefore return to " normal work " the following morning. But in the provinces the workers had taken over a number of radio stations, and news of a very different kind was being beamed from them.

There were now hundreds of Workers' Councils throughout the country. The number of people in the Councils varied considerably. So did their programmes. But all included demands for the abolition of the A.V.O., for the complete withdrawal of Russian troops, for political and civil liberty, for workers' management of factories and industries, for independent trade unions and freedom for all political parties, and for a general amnesty for all the insurrectionists.

The various programmes also called for improvements in wages and pensions, but nowhere were these the first items on the list. Many included demands for ' parliamentary democracy '. A number expressed their confidence in Nagy.

Before ' revolutionary socialists ' raise their hands in puritan horror, let them remember that in relation to the social, political and economic conditions prevailing in Hungary prior to October 1956, even a Liberal programme would appear revolutionary. In such conditions, democratic slogans have an explosive effect. They were a great step forward. They resulted in the smashing of the totalitarian state machine. These demands had never been realised under the Horthy regime. The Hungarians turned their backs on both the feudal-capitalist dictatorship and on the Stalinists. The workers were not blinded by bourgeois ideology : while they supported broad democratic claims, they also *fought* for claims of their own. The workers wanted no more elections in which the Communist Party imposed a single list of candidates and where the result had been decided in advance. They wanted to choose their representatives themselves. They wanted the one-party system abolished. They had seen it result in the suppression of all opinions and all groupings which did not conform to the views disseminated by those who controlled the State. They wanted freedom to organise themselves. It cannot be doubted that such freedom would have led them to make conscious choices between a number

---

67. Hubert Ripka, *Eastern Europe in the Post War World*, p.166.

of revolutionary parties or groups, and to reject both bourgeois and bureaucratic parties which could have threatened their freedom. Their reactions were fundamentally sound. Even their demand for freedom of the press was aimed at the destruction of organs owing allegiance to the State.

A revolution is never 'pure'. Different tendencies show themselves. The great revolution of 1917 was not pure—side by side with the workers and poor peasants there fought sections of the petty bourgeoisie . . . and even some elements who felt indignant at the Czar's inability effectively to wage the war against Germany. When revolution breaks out in the so-called Peoples' Democracies or in the U.S.S.R., the forces at work will be particularly complex. Totalitarianism gives rise to universal feelings of revolt. The majority of the population will some day line up against it, bound at first by a common objective : freedom. After this first stage, some will doubtless want to revive the religion of their ancestors, archaic national customs, the little private profits they had once made. Others will want radical social change and will seek to bring about the society to which their rulers had paid lip service (while they went about destroying any attempt to achieve it). Shopkeepers will thank God for lower taxes. They may even seek to raise their prices. The workers meanwhile will be forming their Councils and will take over the factories.

* * *

The level of political consciousness achieved by the Hungarian workers was quite astonishing. For twelve years every means of propaganda had been used to stuff their minds with the myths and dogmas of the Party's infallibility, of its right to rule 'on behalf of the working class'. But the workers knew they had remained a subject class. They had remained those who merely carried out the self-interested decisions taken by a managerial and bureaucratic hierarchy. The most 'revolutionary' words were no substitute for the reality of their everyday experience both in production and in society at large. Reality, however fogged by incessant propaganda, kept their class instinct unblunted.

On Thursday, the Councils had begun to link up. In the cities, the main Councils (usually simply called ' Revolutionary Councils ') consisted of delegates from all the councils in the area. Some of these Revolutionary Councils included representatives from white-collar workers, from the local peasants and from the army. Peasants willingly supplied the rebels with food. In some agricultural areas, despite their allegedly intrinsic conservatism, the peasants formed their own councils —for example, that of the big state farm at Babolna.[68]

By Thursday afternoon, while Nagy and Kadar were promising they would negotiate for the withdrawal of the Russians, it had become clear that nothing could stop the growth of

68. For an account of the Babolna Peasants' Council, see Peter Fryer— *Hungarian Tragedy*, pp.60-62.

the Councils and of the General Strike. By the evening the Councils constituted the only real power in the country apart from the Red Army.[69] Radio Budapest meanwhile paternalistically proclaimed : " The Government knows that the rebels are quite sincere."

Thursday, October 25, marked a sort of turning point. It seemed the Government was giving way. Premier Nagy now appeared to realise the strength of the movement throughout the country. The previous morning he had only appealed to the " People of Budapest ". At that time Revolutionary Councils had already been formed in all the main cities. The Miskolc Revolutionary Council had, for example, been elected early on Wednesday by all the workers of the factories in the area. It immediately organised a strike in all sectors except the public services (transport, electrical power supply and hospitals). A delegation was sent to the capital to co-ordinate activities with the Budapest Councils, and there to put forward the proposals of the Miskolc Council's programme. These proposals were similar to those mentioned above. They had been made known to the whole of Hungary on Thursday 25 when the revolutionaries had gained control of Miskolc Radio.

The Miskolc Council was not opposed to Nagy. It even proposed him as First Minister of a new government. But that did not prevent it from doing the opposite of what Nagy wanted. When he begged the insurrectionaries to lay down their arms and go back to work, the Miskolc Council formed workers' militias, maintained and extended the strike and organised itself as a local government independent of the central power. . . It was only ready to support Nagy if he applied a revolutionary programme. Thus when Nagy brought representatives of the Smallholders Party (Zoltan Tildy and Bela Kovacs) into the Government the council reacted vigorously. In a special communiqué broadcast on Saturday 27, at 9.30 p.m., the Council declared that it had " taken power in all the Borsod region.[70] It severely condemns all those who term our battle a battle against the will and power of the people. We have confidence in Imre Nagy, but we do not agree with the composition of his Government. All those politicians who have sold themselves to the Soviet Union must not have a place in the Government.

" This last declaration also puts the activity of the Council into proper perspective. It acted like an autonomous gov-

---

69. Even the bureaucrats of U.N.O. recognised this. A U.N. special committee report on Hungary stated: " The Workers' Councils emerged from the Revolution as the only organisations commanding the support of the overwhelming majority of the people and in a position to require the government to negotiate with them, because they constituted a force able to bring about the resumption of work."

70. North-East Hungary, on the borders of Czechoslovakia. Coal mines and steel works amongst the most important in the country. Large power station, iron-smelting, and centre of the Hungarian chemical industry.

ernment. On the day it took power in the Borsod region, it dissolved the organisations which were the hallmark of the preceding regime, that is, all the organisations of the Communist Party. This measure was announced by the radio on the morning of Sunday, October 28. It also announced that the peasants in the region had driven out those responsible for the kolkhozes and begun a redistribution of the land. In Györ, in Pecs, in the greater part of other large towns, the situation was similar to that in Miskolc. It was the Workers' Councils which directed everything : they armed the fighters, organised the provisioning, presented the political and economic demands."[71]

* * *

Some idea as to what the Revolutionary Councils were like can be got by looking at the Council at Györ. Its headquarters were the Town Hall. At almost any time of the day, the square outside was packed with groups of people deeply, and often loudly, engrossed in discussion. In a revolution 'from below', there will always be a great deal of talking, arguing, row, jostling, polemic, excitement and agitation.

Delegations leaving the Town Hall for other Councils crossed deputations coming in from the various local groups and committees. The noise and bustle inside the Town Hall reminded one of the seeming chaos of a disturbed ants nest. Shouldered rifles got caught up with shouldered flags. Arm-banded people holding documents jostled their way through thronged corridors. People filled the rooms. As one walked along the corridors one knew from the various sounds coming from the rooms that this was a real people's movement—a calm male voice, the shrill ring of a telephone, the excited tones of a girl, uproar, laughter, booing, swearing, applause. Many deputations demanded lorries for a great attack on Budapest to relieve Red Army pressure on the 'freedom fighters'. Council members argued that this would prejudice the success of the revolution. All lorries that could be spared should be used to carry food to the people of Budapest. The huge numbers of people who turned out to help with this operation showed that a majority agreed with the Council's decision. Meanwhile a man was addressing a crowd in the square demanding the removal of the 'compromisers' from the Council. The spokesman of a deputation wanting a 'march on Budapest' was denouncing those on the Council who wanted 'to pacify us instead of mobilising us'. But from this seeming chaos had nevertheless evolved a programme of demands which had the support of the great majority.

From the first day of the revolution, a truly proletarian movement had expressed itself in the spontaneous formation of Councils all over Hungary. These Councils, partially isolated by the Red Army, immediately sought to federate.

71. Quoted from *Socialisme ou Barbarie*, Vol. IV, No. 20, pp. 90-91.

By the end of the first week, they had virtually established a Republic of Councils. Only *their* authority meant anything. The Government, regardless of the fact that Nagy was at its head, had no authority whatsoever.

Does anyone still wonder why the Kremlin and its stooges used the foullest methods to smear and discredit this Revolution ? They called it a ' counter-revolution ', a ' fascist uprising '.[72] Does anyone still wonder why the press and the ' leaders ' of the West used lies in their efforts to misrepresent this Revolution as merely a ' national ' uprising ? Nationalist aspects there certainly were, but these were taken out of context and given a prominence and an importance they certainly did not warrant.[73]

* * *

Apart from the industrial workers the real social force in the provinces was the agricultural proletariat—the peasantry. Peasant claims during this period may have been confused, but their struggle for the division of the land had a revolutionary character. To get rid of the Kolkhoze (collective farm) bosses, had for them the same meaning as getting rid of the great landowners. Under the Horthy regime, agricultural workers represented over 40% of the population. They had tasted the benefits of agrarian reform after the war, but saw themselves almost immediately deprived of their new rights and forced into collective farms. Hatred for the bureaucrats who managed the co-operatives and got rich at their expense came to replace, almost without transition, the hatred they had previously felt for their ancestral exploiters—the landed aristocrats.

After October 23, a redistribution of land took place in some districts. In others the co-operatives continued to function although taken over by the peasants. This suggests that certain peasant groups were aware of the advantages of collective work despite the exploitation they had suffered under the Rakosi regime. Although many peasants were prepared to put their trust in representatives of parties such as the Smallholders (who reflected and expressed their religious and family traditions) they nevertheless remained members of an exploited class. They showed they were ready to reunite with the working class in its struggle for socialist aims.

In this context, the programme of the Magyarovar Municipal Executive Committee, (a body obviously directed by peasant elements) should be mentioned. It demanded

---

72. " Counter-revolution in Hungary staged an uprising in the hours of darkness on Tuesday night." [*Daily Worker*, October 25, 1956.] The same edition ran an article entitled "The Hell that was Horthy's", thus implying that the current revolt was of fascist nature.

73. In his book *A Handful of Ashes*, Noel Barber of the *Daily Mail* quotes what he calls " the demands of the Writers' Union " (pp. 89-90). His words bear little relation to the original text. For example, he makes absolutely no mention of workers' management or workers' control.

free elections under the control of the United Nations, the immediate re-establishment of the professional organisation of the peasantry, and the free exercise of their profession by small craftsman and tradesmen. The programme goes on to make a whole series of bourgeois-democratic claims. But at the same time it demands " the suppression of all class distinctions " (point 13). This surely shows that within the peasantry conservative and revolutionary elements always co-exist. This had been shown by the Russian Revolution itself, some 40 years earlier.

While the idea of collective farms could be profoundly socialist, collective ownership only has a socialist content provided the association of peasants is freely arrived at. If, as was the case prior to October 23, agricultural workers are forced into collectives, if they do not themselves determine their work in common but have to carry out orders of officials who don't work, if their standard of living does not increase, if the differentials between their incomes and those of the bureaucracy are great and grow greater, then such collectives have nothing whatever to do with socialism. They can in fact prove to be instruments for a ' rationalised ' and intensified form of exploitation.

The Revolutionary Programme

"Proletarian revolutions . . . again and again stop short in their progress ; retrace their steps in order to make a fresh start ; are pitilessly scornful of the half-measures, the weaknesses, the futility of their preliminary essays. It seems as if they had overthrown their adversaries only in order that these may draw renewed strength from contact with the earth and return to the battle like giants refreshed. Again and again they shrink back apalled before the vague immensity of their own ends."
K. Marx. *The Eighteenth Brumaire of Louis Bonaparte* (1852).

On Friday October 26, the newly formed National Council of Free Trade Unions published its famous resolution. This Council was a federation of the recently dissolved and reformed trade unions.

The resolution comprised a list of far-ranging demands. It gathered together and clarified the demands put forward by various Workers Councils throughout the country. It was signed by the President of the Council. The demands were as follows:

" *Political*
(1) That the fighting cease, an amnesty be declared, and negotiations begun with the Youth delegates.
(2) That a broad government, comprising representatives of the Trade Unions and of youth, be constituted with Imre Nagy as its president.
(3) That the country's economic situation be put to the people in all honesty.
(4) That help be given to people wounded in the tragic battles which had just taken place and to the families of the victims.
(5) That, to maintain order, the police and the army be reinforced by a national guard composed of workers and young people.
(6) That, with the support of the trade unions, an organisation of young workers be formed.
(7) That the new government start immediate negotiations for the withdrawal of Russian troops from Hungarian territory.

Economic

(1) Constitution of Workers' Councils in all the factories, to establish (a) workers' management and (b) a radical transformation of the system of central planning and direction of the economy by the state.

(2) Readjustment of wages: immediate rise of 15% in monthly wages less than 800 forints and of 10% in wages less than 1,500 forints. Maximum monthly wages to be fixed at 3,500 forints.

(3) Abolition of production norms except in factories where the workers' council elect to keep them.

(4) Abolition of the 4% tax paid by unmarried people and childless families.

(5) The lowest pensions to be increased.

(6) Family allowances to be increased.

(7) Speed-up of house building by the State.

(8) That the promise made by Imre Nagy be kept regarding the start of negotiations with the Government of the U.S.S.R. and other countries with a view to establishing economic relations ensuring mutual advantages by adhering to the principle of equality."[74]

The resolution concluded by demanding that the Hungarian trade unions should function as before 1948, and should henceforth be called: The Free Hungarian Trade Unions.

The *Daily Worker* of Saturday, October 27, 1956, significantly ignored the political demands, but published an approximately correct version of all eight economic ones. The economic points of the programme alone must have startled *Daily Worker* readers who simultaneously were being told that the revolution 'owed its inspiration to fascism'. The newspaper of the British Communist Party presumably took its line from *Pravda*.[75] The Kremlin mouthpiece, echoed the words of Shepilov, the Russian Foreign Minister, when it reported: "Events in Hungary have amply demonstrated that a reactionary, counter-revolutionary underground, well-armed and thoroughly trained for vigorous action against the people's system, had been set up there with help from outside . . . (but) it is clear that People's Hungary had, and has now, a number of difficulties and unsolved problems. There have been serious mistakes in the economic field . . . "[76]

But why did the *Daily Worker* keep so silent about the political demands of the National Council of Free Trade Unions ? Undoubtedly, because the programme as a whole was further indisputable proof of what the real forces were behind the Revolution.

Although the Hungarian workers still saw the problem in

74. Quoted from *Socialisme ou Barbarie*—vol. IV, No. 20, p.92.
75. The *Daily Worker's* special correspondent in Budapest, Peter Fryer, had his dispatches mutilated beyond recognition by the Editor and finally suppressed altogether.
76. *Daily Worker*, October 29, 1956.

terms of 'men of good will' in whom they could have confidence, they were sufficiently alive to the inadequacies of this view to demand that direct representatives of workers and youth be included in the Government, and that the Government be supported by the permanent arming of the youth and of the workers. Youth was undoubtedly the vanguard of the Revolution.

The Hungarian unions moreover were not prepared to leave to the Government the job of deciding everything in their name. Through their demand for the recognition of their own autonomous organisations (free, democratically-elected and truly representative of the class), they wanted to consolidate and extend the power they already held. Hence their demand for the "constitution of Workers' Councils in all factories". They may not have been aware of the implications of their demands and of their potential power to enforce them. Yet the trend was clear. In their everyday lives, in their work, they were not prepared to remain mere executants. They wanted to act on their own behalf.

For proof, let us look again at the first 'economic' point, which demanded the establishment of workers' management and a radical transformation of the system of central planning and direction of the economy by the State. The demand may be imprecisely formulated, but we can understand its basic logic. Workers were rejecting the idea that production should be planned independently of them. They were rejecting the State bureaucracy's 'right' to send down the instructions. They were intensely interested in *what* was to be decided nationally—and by whom; in *what* industries or what sections of industry the biggest efforts would have to be made — and why; *what* was to be the volume of production in each section and *how* production was to be organised. They wanted to know how all this would affect their standard of living, the length of their working week, and the rhythm of work it would all entail.

The basic logic of the first demand is reinforced by the second and third. We can have no doubt about what was really in the minds of the workers. The demand that production norms be abolished (except in the factories where the Councils elected to keep them) is quite precise. It emphasises an elementary point : since the workers are the producers, they must be free to organise their work as they understand it. They wished to be rid of the whole hierarchical set-up of the bureaucracy: from those at its summit, who took the key decisions about the level of production down through the 'office scientists', with their charts and graphs, seeking to interpret these decisions — down further still to the foremen and time-and-motion snoopers, on the shop floor, with their stop-watches, hustling the workers to make products out of blueprints. In all of these the workers saw attempts to dominate the labour process from the outside, attempts to subordinate human work to that of the machine — often to a point where the effort required was too great even for the machine itself.

It is characteristic of the managerial bureaucrats, both East and West, that they seek to maintain and widen a hierarchy among the workers. This, indeed, is essential to management. Only in this way can they hope to exercise a more complete control over 'their' labour force. The demand for a readjustment of wages was made to counteract this tendency. The Hungarian workers were quite aware that a wide range of pay scales (sometimes very complicated) enabled their rulers, on the one hand, to foster the growth of a 'labour aristocracy' which would support the established regime, and on the other hand, to divide the workers, to isolate them from one another.

This struggle against hierarchy and wage differentials is fundamental for any movement seeking to achieve workers' power and a classless society. It can be seen to emerge, in the United States, Britain, France or Germany, whenever 'unofficial' strikes occur independently of the union leadership. To maintain its control, management seeks to sectionalise the managed. But in so doing it creates enormous problems for itself. As all this becomes clearer to the workers, as inevitably it must, the struggle becomes sharper. Due to the speed of modern technological development and to the ever-increasing division of labour, workers whose jobs once appeared to be different are now beginning to see that they are not as different as all that. Wage differentials (or, for the moment at least, their more extreme instances) begin to appear absurd.

The trade unions' resolution clearly revealed (and this is its great importance) that the Hungarian workers had discovered that under the rule of the bureaucracy, they had as little say in the running of their own affairs as they had had under private capitalism. They saw the real division in their industries, in their society, and in their lives, as the one between those who decided everything and those who had only to obey. A mere three days after the rising and still in the fire of battle, their programme was an affirmation of all they were fighting for. It was a fundamentally revolutionary programme, although they had little idea of how it was to be carried out.

This new federation of trade unions, shorn of the bureaucratic leadership, democratically elected and basing itself on the Workers' Councils and their demands, was typical of the Hungarian political scene in those last days of October 1956. Freedom became an elixir, gulped down greedily by those who had been dying of thirst. The people seemed to sense that this freedom was to be short-lived, so ardently did they go about re-arranging everything around them.

Dual Power

" What constitutes dual power ? The fact that
by the side of the Provisional Government, the
government of the bourgeoisie, there has
developed another, as yet weak, embryonic, but
undoubtedly real and growing government—the
Soviets of Workers and Soldiers Deputies . . .
a power based not on laws made by a centralised
state power, but on outright revolutionary
seizure, on the direct initiative of the masses
from below."
V. I. Lenin. *On Dual Power* (April 1917).

Several parties suddenly re-appeared, including the Social-
Democratic Party, the National Peasant Party and the Smallholders Party. Kadar disclosed that the Communist Party
had been ' re-organised '. It was to have a new name : the
Socialist Workers' Party. The new Executive Committee
would only be composed of those who had fought against
Rakosi (himself, Nagy and five others !).

Twenty-five new dailies replaced the five dreary and
obedient mouthpieces of the defunct ' people's bureaucracy '.
Not only did people get news, real news at last, but also
clashes of opinion, full-blooded polemics, hard-hitting com-
mentaries, satire and wit.

But there was little to be gay about in Budapest. Day and
night, gunfire could be heard. There was no public transport.
Knocked-out Russian tanks stood raggedly about the streets,
while others rumbled continually up and down. Shattered
buildings with gaping holes cast grotesque shadows across
hundreds of bodies lying in the streets amid the broken glass,
empty cartridges and other debris. Occasionally, a van with
a Red Cross flag or a lorry-load of ' freedom fighters ' would
go crunching by. Some food shops were open. The cinemas,
theatres and restaurants were closed. In the ferment of
activity, there was no time or thought for entertainment.

From Friday night on, the struggle had become increasingly
bitter. By this time, 5,500 political prisoners had been released
by the revolutionaries. During the night of Saturday to
Sunday, the ' boys ' broke into Budapest prison and released
all the political prisoners. Their poor physical condition and
the nauseating stories they told of torture by the A.V.O.,
heightened the peoples' hatred for the secret police. This,
coupled with the fact that only the A.V.O. fought with the
Red Army, brought the people's anger to a climax. Almost
every captured A.V.O. man was beaten to death and hanged
by the feet, to be spat upon by the angry crowds.

Budapest Radio was still calling for a cease-fire. Again and again it repeated Kadar's and Nagy's promises. They promised immediate wage increases. They promised the formation of Workers' Councils in all factories. (Since every factory already had its Workers' Council, this was a sinister offer indeed). They also promised an immediate start of negotiations to put Russo-Hungarian relations on a basis of equality. But they added that none of these things would be done until 'law and order' was restored. Throughout, 'law and order' remained Nagy's refrain.

Whom did Nagy want to impress with his demands for 'order'? The workers? He was quite aware of what was happening up and down the country. He knew that delegates from the main committees throughout Hungary had met in Györ to co-ordinate and put forward the people's demands. These now included "withdrawal of Hungary from the Warsaw Pact". The presence in Györ of delegates from Budapest probably gave credence to the report that a provisional government was being formed there. Nagy had to get some 'influential' support quickly.

Nagy went to Budapest Radio again. (All other radio stations in the country — Miskolc, Györ, Pecs, Szeged, Debrecen and Magyaróvár — were now controlled by the Revolutionary Councils). He announced some concessions. The A.V.O. would be dissolved. The Government would be 're-organised'.

A cease-fire was promised while the Government 're-organisation' was in progress. By this time, a number of fighting groups had surrendered, because their ammunition had run out. Others, weakened by casualties, had been rounded up. But at several points, notably Szena Square and the Killian Barracks, groups were still holding out. By the weekend many people began to think the Revolution had gained some kind of victory. Russian tanks were no longer attacking. There were rumours that they were about to withdraw from Budapest.

Yet the workers were suspicious of Nagy. His various pronouncements about 'order' and so on, seemed to them deliberate delaying tactics, aimed at getting a tighter grip on the country. On Monday, October 29, delegates from Councils throughout the country, meeting at Györ, sent Nagy a strongly worded resolution, re-affirming their demands. This message almost amounted to an ultimatum.

Early on Tuesday morning, Budapest Radio confirmed that the Red Army was to withdraw. Later in the afternoon a statement that "the withdrawal of the troops of the Soviet Union has begun", was broadcast in the name of the Prime Minister. At the same time, Nagy said that "to ensure complete orderliness of the troops' departure, every citizen must refrain from any provocative, disturbing or hostile action". He also appealed for a resumption of work.

Similar appeals were broadcast the same day by Tildy and Kadar.

Red Army units began withdrawing from Budapest at 4 p.m. The workers remained suspicious. The Councils' delegates at Györ immediately put out a call for the General Strike to be maintained and strengthened[77] until the last Russian soldier had left the country. A resumption of work would only be considered when negotiations were started on the basis of their other claims.

* * *

The country was still locked in strike when an official statement was issued that it was not Imre Nagy but András Hegedüs and Ernö Gerö who bore full responsibility for calling in Russian troops on the previous Wednesday morning. At a time when Nagy's authority and that of his ' Government ' were at their lowest, they decided to disclaim all responsibilty for one of the most important events of the whole period : the invoking of the Warsaw Pact ! But Nagy gave no reason for his seven-day silence on this matter. The fact did not escape the notice of the Hungarian workers. A few days earlier they might have been impressed. Now, the strike continued.

As far as the Hungarian people were concerned, with each day that passed the statement assumed a diminishing significance. It was now irrelevant. But it was relevant to the ' leadership '. It showed their dilemma. They were desperate to regain their authority, to re-establish their ' order ' and control. Who knows exactly how far they were successful ? Many intellectuals welcomed Nagy's statement, like drowning men clutch at a straw. They took Nagy back into their hearts. The Government regained some of its authority. A large proportion of the Army and ordinary police began once again to obey its orders. As instructed, they took over, unopposed, from the Russian units withdrawing from Budapest.

On the other hand, the workers in parts of Budapest and in the rest of the country remained armed and solidly behind their own organisations. A classical situation of ' dual power ' existed.

The Hungarian people were weakened at an extremely critical time by the Government's frantic desire to regain control. The Red Army had only withdrawn to positions outside Budapest ! The city was ringed with Russian tanks. At the same time, fresh Russian troops were pouring into the country from the north-east. By Thursday, November 1, (when British aircraft were busy bombing Egyptians at Suez) these new Red Army units had already reached Szolnok, in central Hungary. They were about eighty miles from Budapest.

As soon as the Revolutionary Councils, Workers' Councils

---

77. There had already been a resumption of work in some factories. Public transport had started running again on Saturday, October 27.

and other autonomous organisations in North-east Hungary (e.g. Miskolc) learned about these Russian troop movements, they informed all other Councils throughout the country. Ultimatums were sent to Nagy that unless Red Army soldiers immediately stopped entering Hungary and withdrew, the Councils would take drastic action. This clearly implied that the people themselves would try to stop them.

The Councils received no official answer. Several ministers of Nagy's re-organised Government again appealed for 'order' and for a resumption of work. The strike was now gripping the few hitherto functioning sections of industry. " The workers reiterated : first the Russians must leave, then they would end the strike."[78]

By the evening of November 1, Nagy was under very great pressure indeed. The Hungarian Government delegation — which included Pal Maléter, the well-liked Communist of Killian Barracks fame, who was now Minister of Defence, and General Istvan Kovacs his Chief of Staff — were still nego-tiating with Kremlin representatives about Red Army withdrawal and other military arrangements. The Russians issued a statement that the troops entering Hungary were there simply to cover their withdrawal. But Nagy was now well aware of the Kremlin's purpose. He knew what the fresh Russian divisions were for. He was desperate.

Just before 7 p.m., Prime Minister Imre Nagy, who earlier in the day had taken over the Foreign Ministry, broadcast a short speech in which he declared the neutrality of the ' Hungarian People's Republic '. Nagy had moved a long way towards meeting the demands of the revolutionaries. On October 24, he had invoked the Warsaw Pact. On November 1, he revoked it. But it was too late.

The next day, Friday November 2, the Russian delegate at the United Nations declared that all reports about Russian troops moving back into Hungary were " utterly unfounded ". Most of the Western delegates had a rough idea of the real situation in Hungary. Reports from various radio stations controlled by the revolutionaries had been picked up by Western monitoring services on the Continent, in the United Kingdom and in the U.S.A. Yet neither then nor later did Western delegates 'embarrass' the U.S.S.R. by questioning the truth of its delegate's statement. How could they ? The American Secretary of State, John Foster Dulles, had summed up their attitude eleven days earlier (October 22). In a speech in Washington, he defended the legality of Russian troops being in Poland under the Warsaw Pact: " From the stand-point of international law and violation of treaties, I do not think you could claim that it would be a violation of a treaty."[79]

---

78. George Mikes, *The Hungarian Revolution*, p.145.
79. *New York Times*, October 23, 1956.

At 2.18 p.m. on Saturday, November 3, Radio Budapest announced " the Soviet delegation has promised that no further trains carrying troops will cross the Hungarian frontier ". This promise may well have been kept. Red Army units had by now occupied air fields, main road junctions and railway stations in almost the whole of the country apart from the big cities.

Later in the afternoon, four of Nagy's ministers — Kadar, Apro, Marosán and Münnich — disappeared. They were in fact at the Russian Embassy to which they had been invited for a meeting with Mikoyan, recently flown in from Moscow. Many members of Nagy's latest Government were confident the Russians were not going to attack. Even Pal Maléter, leader of the Hungarian delegation still negotiating at Red Army headquarters, is said to have " trusted their words and sincerity ". On the same day two ministers, Dr. Zolton Tildy, Minister of State, and Geza Losconczi held a press conference in the Gobelin room at Parliament House, Questioned about the imminence of a new Russian attack. Tildy said, " Such a tragedy is humanly impossible . . . it will never take place."

The workers did not share this optimism. The General Strike was now complete. The workers were really in control. If Nagy was really any different from the rest, now was the chance to show it. An appeal from Nagy for the workers to stand fast would have galvanised the revolutionaries. Instead Nagy appealed to . . . U.N.O. !

Just before midnight, Colonel Pal Maléter and General Kovacs were arrested by Red Army officers while officially still taking part in ' negotiations '. They were imprisoned in a villa on Gorky Allée. The scene was set.

The Second Russian Intervention

" Will Hungary move further forward toward Socialism, or will she allow the forces of reaction to gain the upper hand and restore a scheme of things that would throw the nation back a generation ?"
Pravda, November 4, 1956.

At 4 o'clock on Sunday morning, November 4, Budapest was roused by the thunder of shells bursting in the city centre. Hundreds of guns in the hills of Buda opened fire, their flashes flood-lighting the MIG fighters, as they screamed over the city. The armed forces of the Russian State had begun their attack to crush the Hungarian workers.

The attack was country-wide and simultaneous. All the major cities were pounded by artillery. But the people were not terrorised. They knew that the uneasy truce of the last few days wouldn't last. They knew that. militarily, the situation was hopeless. Yet at the first sound of gunfire they were galvanised into action. Young and old, workers, students, soldiers and children, all took up their positions in the streets before the armoured divisions had reached the outskirts of Budapest. The barricades were rebuilt, at times with the same materials used on October 24. In some places children loaded handcarts with suitable objects and dragged them to the barricade builders.

The Russian tanks entered Budapest, their guns blazing. They were firing phosphorus as well as ordinary shells. Several buildings were soon in flames. The tanks were immediately attacked by the people. Pitched battles were fought with the inevitable outcome. The tanks advanced towards the town centre. The struggle was repeated in the other large towns of Hungary. Györ, for example, was completely surrounded by a steel wall of tanks, squeezing in relentlessly. Everywhere, the people fought even more courageously and against far greater odds than ten days earlier. There were now fifteen Russian armoured divisions in the country, with six thousand tanks. Who could still deny this was a popular revolution ?

At 6 a.m. Nagy, with fifteen others and their families, sought refuge in the Yugoslav Embassy, where it had earlier been agreed they would be given protection. Just after

7 a.m., the first Russian tanks reached Parliament Square. Obviously acting on orders, a number of officers rushed into the Parliament Building. They found no one to arrest.

In the streets, between the tall buildings, the din of battle was becoming deafening. Smoke from burning buildings, exploding shells and Molotov cocktails, mixed with the dust from crashing masonry to create a choking fog. The sight of the mounting dead and the agonising cries of the wounded created a fog to choke the mind. Was this nightmare a 'defence of socialism'?

As the tanks continued their advance, strong points of resistance emerged : Szena Square and the Killian Barracks as in the earlier battles. The single field gun by the Corvin Cinema was still in action. At several points near the old Royal Palace in Buda, along the Boulevard and at the Polytechnic, the revolutionaries could not be dislodged.

Despite very heavy bombardment, all the big working class districts — particularly 'red' Czepel, Dunapentele, Ujpest, Köbanya — were still in the hands of the workers.[80] In the first Russian attack, these working class areas had been subjected to lighter treatment. Now, they bore the full weight of the onslaught. The new Russian troops had no sentimental feelings about Hungarians. They had been well indoctrinated: the freedom fighters were 'fascists' and 'bourgeois capitalists'. Peter Fryer, in his last dispatch to the *Daily Worker* (which the editor would not even allow his staff to see) says : " Some of the rank-and-file Soviet troops have been telling people that they had no idea they had come to Hungary. They thought at first they were in Berlin, fighting German fascists."[81] These new troops were disgruntled at having to come to Hungary. Some were frightened, not only by the sight of so many of their tanks standing burnt-out and silent, but by the ferocity and courage of the Hungarians. Hand-to-tank fighting was going on in many streets. People ran up close to the tanks and made sure their Molotov cocktails did not miss—it is difficult for a tank to train its guns on a close target. Some got so close to the tanks that they were able to throw in hand-grenades, then close the driver's hatch.

The fight of the Hungarian workers should be remembered by those who say the British working class has been completely demoralised by their rulers' well-propagated ideology of 'self'. In Hungary, years of violent suppression and concentrated propaganda had failed to destroy the workers' vision of a new society. They were fighting what they knew to be a military force a thousand times more powerful than themselves. But they were fighting for something more than bread and circuses. They were fighting for a totally

---

80. The *Daily Worker* of November 5, reported that Kadar had "called for the arming of the workers in the factories."
81. Peter Fryer, *Hungarian Tragedy*, p.85.

new way of life. In a mere eleven days they had become giants.

At this stage Janos Kadar came forward to help the Kremlin put the clock back. At Szolnok, sixty miles south-east of Budapest, Kadar formed what he called a new Workers' and Peasants' Government.[82] This Government immediately issued a proclamation. It had asked the Russian Government "for help in liquidating the counter-revolutionary forces and restoring order ". The *Daily Worker* of November 5 had put it slightly differently : " It called for Soviet aid to close the Austro-Hungarian border across which fascist elements had been streaming for several days."[83] This all appeared an underestimation of the ' wisdom ' of the Russian Government, which had started to ' help in liquidating ' the Revolution several hours before the Kadar Government had even been formed ! Kadar's part was that of an ' accessory after the fact ' pretending he was speaking before the fact. Either way, Kadar and the others were guilty of complicity. They carry a full share of responsibilty for the savage and brutal massacre of thousands of workers and young people in Hungary.

The Kremlin remained consistent in its lies and hypocrisy. Later in the day, while mass murder continued, the Russian delegate, Sobelev, calmly addressed a meeting of the United Nations Security Council. " Events in Hungary ", he said, " have clearly shown that the workers there, who had been able to make great achievements under a democratic regime, had rightly raised a number of questions appertaining to the eradication of certain shortcomings in their economic life. But they were exploited by reactionary, counter-revolutionary elements who wanted to undermine the popular regime and restore the former landlord and capitalist regime in Hungary."[84]

Goebbels claimed that " the bigger the lie, the more it's believed ". He never bettered this one. The workers were leading a Revolution against a ' democratic regime ' which had given them ' great achievements ' ? They had raised ' questions ' about ' shortcomings in their economic life ' ? Demands become ' questions '. Total exploitation becomes ' shortcomings ' ! Note again the fear of admitting, no

---

82. The four principal Ministers were : Foreign Minister, Imre Horvath; Deputy Prime Minister, Ferenc Münnich; Minister of Defence and Interior, Antal Apro; Minister of Agriculture, Imre Degoe. Two Social Democrats were also given Ministries : Minister of State, Gyorgy Morosan and Minister of Trade, Sandor Ronai.

83. In the same issue, the front page headlines ran : "New Hungarian Anti-fascist Government in Action—Soviet Troops called in to stop White Terror." Further down the page the *Daily Worker* reported : " Budapest Radio, under control of the Kadar Government, said that Ernö Gerö, former First Secretary of the Hungarian Workers' Party had been murdered in a ' barbarous fashion ' by the rebels." In fact Gerö had been taken to Moscow by the Russians on October 24.

84. *Daily Worker*, November 5, 1956.

matter how guardedly, the existence of political dissatisfaction ! And does the workers' programme look like that of a people bent on restoring capitalism and led by ' reactionary and counter-revolutionary elements ' ?

' Counter-revolution ' was the propaganda bogey of the day. Just after midday on Sunday, November 4, Moscow Radio announced that the " counter-revolution in Hungary has been crushed ". Later in the afternoon, the Kremlin broadcast that the " complete defeat of the counter-revolution is under way ". At 8 p.m. Kadar announced that the " counter-revolution " had been completely defeated. Following Kadar, Moscow Radio reverted to its midday statement declaring that " order has been restored in Hungary and the resistance of a negligible handful overcome with the assistance of the Budapest population."[85] In fact, heavy fighting was to continue for about ten days.

What did the Kremlin mean by " counter-revolution " ? Through careful propaganda over the years they had sustained the myth that despite their tactical zig-zags, theirs were still the original revolutionary aims of October 1917. Members and supporters of the various communist parties have been led to revere the Soviet Union as the vanguard and guardian of this revolution. Any movement that opposed Russian ' socialism ' was branded as ' counter-revolutionary '. This was just one of the many smears used by the Russian bureaucracy to discredit those who fundamentally challenged its rule. The Hungarian revolutionaries believed they were fighting for a society in which the basic conflict in production and social life had been removed — for a classless society in which the people themselves managed their factories, their industries and thus their lives. They had had their illusions in Russia savagely dispelled during the previous twelve years. No one has done more than the Hungarians to expose the myth of Russia as the vanguard of such a revolution and of such a society. They exposed it with their political and economic organisation. They exposed with their revolutionary demands. They exposed it in a grim battle with the Red Army. Above all, they exposed it with their humour.

Out of their misery came an incredible and heart-rending humour. It emphasised rather than disguised the people's bitterness. As all major resistance drew to its close, a week after the second Russian attack, hundreds of posters, roughly produced and simply worded, began mysteriously to appear on the ruins of Budapest — like smiles through tears. Their irony was crushing. One neatly showed the Hungarians' contempt for Russian smear tactics: " Ten million counter-revolutionaries at large in the country!" Another said: " Former aristocrats, land and factory owners, Cardinals, Generals and other supporters of the old capitalist regime, disguised as factory workers and peasants are making propa-

---

85. *Daily Worker*, November 5, 1956.

ganda against the patriotic government and against our Russian friends." Another recalled a phrase from pre-revolution travel propaganda: "Come and see our beautiful capital in Soviet-Hungarian friendship month." A skit on the Government and its spate of propaganda about what ' honest ' Hungarians were doing[86] appeared in a little poster which said: "Luckily, seven honest men were found in the country. They are all in the Government."

During the week, this puppet Government took up the old Stalinist tactic of blowing hot and cold in its psychological war for the minds of the Hungarian people. Kadar kept up a continuous barrage of promises and threats. But it had no effect. The people had been immunised through years of bitter experience. He announced ' changes '. Many members of the A.V.O.—Rakosi's and Gerö's secret police —were still alive. As the Red Army began to take control. they crawled out of their hiding places, like rats from sewers. Kadar, who had already changed the name of the Communist Party to the Hungarian Socialist Workers' Party. now changed the name of the A.V.O. New names. new uniforms. But they still behaved like the secret police of a totalitarian state. Not only were they eager to act on Kadar's orders. They were burning for revenge. During the last week of October, the workers, enraged by A.V.O. atrocities, had chased them underground. With the Red Army to protect them, they now reverted to their terror methods. Torture and beatings began again. While fierce battles were still raging, freedom fighters were being hanged from the bridges on the Danube and in the streets. Almost all were workers. The bodies, sometimes hanging in groups. had notices pinned to them : "This is how we deal with counter-revolutionaries ".

---

86. This was started by Moscow radio on the afternoon of November 4, which, according to the *Daily Worker* of November 5, announced: " All honest Hungarian patriots are taking an active part . . . in disarming the mutineers and in overcoming individual nests of resistance of fascist groups."

The Proletariat Fights On

"The history of all hitherto existing society is the history of class struggles."
K. Marx and F. Engels. *Manifesto of the Communist Party* (1848).

But the workers were not cowed. Despite Government appeals, threats and terror, the importance of the Workers' Councils, formed in October, increased daily.

The Councils maintained and strengthened the solidarity of the General Strike. Intellectuals, peasants and other non-industrial workers who had not hitherto fully appreciated their importance now turned even more towards them. They recognised that *here* was the heart of real power in the country. Kadar knew it too. The Councils had already shown how efficiently they could run the country. And in the process, Kadar, the Government, the A.V.O., indeed the whole bureaucratic set-up, had been exposed as not only superfluous to the needs of the people, but as an encumbrance holding back their advance to real freedom.

The ruling minorities of the whole world had been given redundancy notices by the workers of Hungary. A new form of society was here being juxtaposed to the old. The rotten-ness of the 'old' was being forced into relief. The shock was not only felt in Moscow. It reverberated through the managing and bureaucratic 'elites' the whole world over. The Hungarian workers had made it quite clear they did not want the 'Communism' of the Kremlin. In so doing, they had made it equally clear that capitalism, even in its 'en-lightened' form, was just as irrelevant to their needs. Most important of all, they had proved once again that the achieve-ment of 'workers' power' and the emancipation of the working class can only come from below, from the workers' own action, and never from a 'leadership' acting on their behalf.

In the conditions of pre-revolution Hungary a movement advocating ideas such as our own would almost certainly have been liquidated. It was just these ideas nevertheless that came to the fore during the last week of October. Several people had no doubt held them for some time. For others, they were born out of the impact and intellectual ferment of the struggle itself, as part of their class instinct and elemental sense of solidarity. A group with views such as ours might have helped, during the revolution, explicitly to formulate these ideas and to warn of the dangers of the bureaucratic counter-revolution. As it was, the ideas emerged clearly enough to gain the allegiance of hundreds and later of thousands and tens of thousands of people. This was a grave threat to the Kadar Government. It was, above all, a threat to the Russian bosses who had 'elected' it . . . with their six thousand tanks. The threat had to be smashed.

* * *

Large-scale military resistance ceased by Saturday, November 10. Scores of disabled Russian tanks lay scattered around Budapest. It had obviously been contrary to accepted military strategy to send so much armour into the built-up areas of a city to suppress a revolution. One reason for the Kremlin's decision may well have been their shocked realisation of how much fraternisation had taken place between Russian troops and the Hungarian people during the first attack.

On November 4, to be sure of success, the Russians felt it necessary to use a large number of troops. They put them in tanks (called 'Kadar taxis' by the Hungarians) to reduce to a minimum physical contact with the civilian people. Russian soldiers would thus see less of Hungarian living conditions, see less that it was ordinary working people they were fighting. Yet they could see the devastation their bombardment was causing in the cities. In his last unpublished dispatch to the *Daily Worker*, Peter Fryer wrote : " I have just come out of Budapest, where for six days I have watched Hungary's new born freedom tragically destroyed by Soviet troops. Vast areas of the city—the working class areas above all—are virtually in ruins. For four days and nights Budapest was under continuous bombardment. I saw a once lovely city battered, bludgeoned, smashed and bled into submission."[87] By the end of that terrible week, a trickle back to work began. But the workers had not submitted. Most sections of industry were still strike-bound.

In the towns, organised resistance by groups of fighting workers and youth ended on November 14. Although sporadic fighting continued well into 1957, in the country districts, the military defeat of the Hungarians was complete. But what everyone had thought would only take a few hours, had taken over a week. And the Hungarian people were still not defeated. The Workers' Councils were gaining strength. They proclaimed that their demands remained unchanged. These were similar to those put forward by the Council of Hungarian Trade Unions—although in some cases there was now more stress on the demand for the 'release' of Nagy and for the withdrawal of Russian troops.

---

87. Peter Fryer. *Hungarian Tragedy*, p.83.

The General Strike continued.

           *   *   *

While the fighting was still raging Kadar began to act against the Workers' Councils. He proceeded cautiously. In terms of active support the Councils had far greater power in the country than had the Government. Kadar made a few selective arrests of members of the Councils' Action Committees. This had little or no effect. Others immediately took their place.

On November 12, 1956, Kadar made more promises. He promised that the secret police would be abolished. He was ready to negotiate with Kremlin representatives about the complete withdrawal of Russian troops. Some of the most-hated Stalinists would be removed from the Party. The people did not believe him. Kadar then announced that twelve lead-ing Stalinists had been expelled from the Party, including Ernö Gerö.[88] This move caused a few workers to return to work. But there was still a partial strike. Industrial activity was not even half-hearted. Public transport was chaotic. The train service was haphazard. When some trams ran in Buda-pest, crowds stopped them and the blackleg crews were chased home. People employed in hospitals remained at work. So did those concerned with food packaging and distribution, but they threatened to strike if there was any large resump-tion of work.

Unsuccessfully, the Kadar Government appealed, threat-ened, begged, making bigger and bigger verbal concessions. The Kremlin sent in more divisions of infantry. It made no difference. The strike, though not total, continued. The Workers' Councils continued to increase their power, which daily showed itself greater than that of the Kadar Govern-ment.

Kadar then appealed directly to the workers to end the strike. He used the bogey argument of rulers everywhere: inflation. They threw his appeal back in his face with a list of further demands: recognition of the Central Council as the negotiating body representing the workers, the release of prisoners, the withdrawal of Russian troops, and the restoration of Nagy as Prime Minister. Although the workers managed most of the factories, these demands showed they knew that their power might eventually be broken by more ruthless methods. They were determined to ' interfere ' for as long as they were able to, and in such

---

88. This appears to contradict the *Daily Worker* report that Gerö had been killed by the rebels on November 4. Perhaps the *Daily Worker's* News Editor, knowing in what kind of esteem Gerö was held by the workers, had made an ' intelligent guess ' about his fate. If so, the *Daily Worker* had been thwarted by the Russians who had ' arrested ' Gerö on October 24, and taken him to Moscow. Gerö was not expelled at this time. On August 19, 1962, the Soviet news agency *Tass* reported that a meeting of the Central Committee of the Hungarian Socialist (Communist) Party had just expelled Gerö—and Rakosi (see *The Guardian*, August 20, 1962, pp.1 and 7).

a way as to leave them with some concrete achievements. The ' release of Nagy ' now featured in all their demands. He had by now become a symbol, rather like Rajk had, earlier in the year, when his rehabilitation had been repeatedly demanded.

A tacit admittance of where real power lay came on Friday, November 16, when Kadar was obliged to start negotiations with the Councils. The delegates from some Councils agreed to ask workers to resume work on condition that a number of their demands were immediately satisfied and the rest later.

At the meeting on November 17, Kadar was told that his appeal had gone out. Workers' delegates then demanded that a National Workers' Council be set up by decree. Kadar said this was unnecessary since there was already a ' Workers' Government ' in Hungary. But he agreed to the recognition of individual Councils and to the establishment of some form of factory militia. He added that if workers' delegates would use their influence to ensure a resumption of work, he would use his to obtain a withdrawal of Russian troops and negotiations between Warsaw Treaty countries about Hungarian neutrality. Workers did not trust this somewhat ambiguous promise. They asked for it to be put in writing. Kadar refused, saying his word should be enough.

The situation was confused. Very few workers resumed work. The negotiations went on fitfully. Precariously, dual power survived.

Towards the end of November, Kadar tried another method to reduce the workers' resistance. As the industrial area of Budapest was the base of this resistance, the peasants were forbidden from bringing food into the area except by permission of the Government. The Red Army saw to it that the order was complied with. At the same time ration cards were issued, but only to workers who reported at the factories. This was clearly an attempt, not merely to starve the workers into submission, but also to drive a wedge between them and the peasants who wanted to sell their produce.

But still the strike continued. The Russians and their puppet Government were becoming increasingly apprehensive about the situation. So much so that, when word got around that the Central Workers' Council of Budapest was to hold a meeting in the National Stadium on November 21, the ' official ' authorities believed the mass meeting would set up another Government, in opposition to Kadar's. This was not only untrue, but quite unnecessary. On November 21, Russian tanks barred the roads leading to the Stadium. The few people already there were dispersed by the A.V.O. In answer to this, the Central Workers' Council called for the strike to be strengthened.

Kadar again appealed for a return to work. Again the

workers renewed their demands. And again they increased the pressure by adding new ones: the formation of a Workers' Militia ; freedom to publish their own uncensored newspaper ; a meeting with Nagy. Kadar reverted to threats. The movement he had earlier referred to as 'a great popular movement', he now called 'counter-revolutionary'—the Workers' Councils were 'fascist-led'! This charge left workers in no doubts as to what was now to happen. In both East and West, a prelude to a successful purge is the raising of a bogey and its denunciation.

The following day, Kadar made his intentions crystal clear. He declared: " . . . a tiger cannot be tamed by baits, it can be tamed and forced to peace only by beating it to death . . . Every worker, instead of *drawing up and scribbling demands* (my italics, A.A.) must immediately and unconditionally begin to work to the best of his ability."

Kadar's attitude merely reflected the Kremlin's, where patience was getting short. The huge army they had in the country was causing them grave problems. Apart from the loss of world prestige entailed in their inability completely to suppress a small country, the oppressed people of Eastern Europe were watching closely. The Kremlin's troops were inadequately fed. Discipline was poor. The longer Russian soldiers stayed in Hungary, the more clearly they perceived the truth. Some had already joined the guerillas in the mountains. Many others had to be disarmed and sent back to Russia, in sealed wagons, because they refused to carry out orders. The Kremlin decided it was now time both to smash the Workers' Councils and to get rid of Nagy.

The Nagy Abduction

Imre Nagy, together with some ex-ministers, high-ranking military personnel and others (including Julia Rajk), had taken refuge in the Yugoslav Embassy. Correspondence between Kadar and the Yugoslav Ambassador, Soldatich, resulted in Kadar guaranteeing the personal safety of Nagy, and both his own safe conduct and that of his group. Then, suddenly, Kadar put forward four conditions :

(1) Nagy's formal resignation as Premier.

(2) A statement from Nagy supporting the Government in its ' fight against counter-revolutionaries '.

(3) Nagy to make a public self-criticism.

(4) Nagy and the rest of the Group to agree to go to one of the ' Peoples' Democracies ' until normality was restored in Hungary.

These conditions were all refused.

Kadar clearly had orders to get Nagy out of the Embassy. He then gave, in writing, an unconditional promise of safe conduct for the group whenever they should decide to leave the Embassy. Some sent messages home, telling relations they were returning. None mentioned the possibility of going to Rumania or any other ' Peoples' Democracy '. A bus was laid on to take them home. At 6.30 on November 23, they all left the Embassy. Soldatich had insisted that two of his Embassy officials should accompany the party. A few hundred yards from the Embassy, the bus was stopped and surrounded by patrol cars. Russian security officers poured out of the cars and into the bus. The Yugoslav officials were ordered to leave, but they refused and were thrown out. The bus was then driven to the Russian Kommandatura.

The Yugoslavs sent strongly-worded notes of protest to Kadar. At first Kadar denied all knowledge of the abduction. He later admitted he knew about it by saying that if Nagy had been allowed to return home, counter-revolutionary elements might have murdered him. He also claimed that Nagy and the others had gone to Rumania at their own request. A likely story. In Rumania the press and radio had for some time shown a more violent hostility to Nagy than in any of the other ' Peoples' Democracies '. An attitude more hostile even than that of the Russians ! How free Nagy's choice had been became evident later, with the news that he and others, including Pal Maléter, had been executed in Rumania.

The Proletariat Crushed

> " The civilisation and justice of bourgeois order
> comes out in its lurid light whenever the slaves
> and drudges of that order rise against their
> masters. Then this civilisation and justice stand
> forth as undisguised savagery and lawless
> revenge . . . a glorious civilisation, indeed, the
> great problem of which is how to get rid of the
> heaps of corpses it made after the battle was
> over !"
> K. Marx. *The Civil War in France* (1871).

On December 2, 1956, *The Observer* reported: " . . . the
(Hungarian) Government's plan to divert Workers' Councils
into innocuous channels by 'legalising' them as organs of
economic self-government, somewhat on the Yugoslav model,
but denying them the right to put forward political demands
or issue a newspaper, has merely led to continued deadlock
in Budapest."

The erratic negotiations between Kadar Government
officials and representatives of the Workers' Councils then
came to an abrupt end. Two prominent members of the
Central Workers' Council were invited to a meeting with
Kadar and his henchmen at the Government Building. They
were the 24-year-old Chairman, Sandor Racs—a pre-October
23 member of the Communist Party and a toolmaker of the
Belajanis Electrical Works in South Buda—and the secretary,
Sandor Bali, a worker from the same factory. On arrival
at the Government Building, they were arrested. All the
workers at the Belajanis factory immediately went on a sit-in
strike. They refused to resume work until their comrades
were released. It was, of course, an 'unofficial' strike.[89]
The factory was seized by hundreds of armed police and
Government militia. In spite of this, the sit-in lasted for
three days, during which time no work was done. Under
the pressure of threats and victimisation the workers were
eventually forced to resume work. Police and militia were
posted all over the factory. Whenever workers gathered to
talk, they were instantly dispersed. Still the workers were

---

89. Before, during and since the period of the Hungarian revolution, all
strikes were 'unofficial' except, perhaps, during the short life of the
National Council of Free Trade Unions, formed in October.

not defeated—they began a ' go-slow '. This, combined with an unplanned campaign of poor-quality individual workmanship, reduced production to 8% of normal. Kadar's comment on these workers was the same as that of managers, politicians and trade union leaders throughout the world—the workers were ' sheep ' led by ' subversive elements '. ' agitators ', ' irresponsible, self-seeking demagogues ', ' spies and agents of Capitalism '. (In the West, for ' Capitalism ' read ' Communism ').

The scene was now set for a full-scale purge of the Workers' Councils. Many prominent committee members were arrested and jailed. This tactic of selective arrests was also applied to many militant student groups. But a reserve of supporters was standing by, ready to step into the breach. When the authorities realised this, widespread arrests of rank-and-file Workers' Council members followed.

A form of passive resistance by the masses then developed, similar to that previously described. It continued for months. I feel this period, beginning in December, 1956, can most graphically be portrayed in diary form : —

December 2, 1956—
Copies of *Népszabadság* (Communist Party newspaper) burned in the streets by crowds, who were later dispersed by Russian troops.

December 4, 1956—
A demonstration by 30,000 women in Budapest, many wearing the national colours of red, white and green (the only way they knew to symbolise their fight for freedom) gathered at the Tomb of the Unknown Warrior in Hero's Square. Russian troops fired over their heads. One woman was hit by a bullet.

December 5, 1956—
Demonstrations numbering many thousands in all parts of the country, including several in Budapest. Another large demonstration of women in Budapest, marched towards the Petőfi statue shouting " Russians go home ! " " We want Nagy ! " " Russian tanks out ! " Some were carrying wreaths and flowers in memory of relations who had been killed. They did not reach the statue, but were intercepted by Russian tanks and infantry. *Nepakarat* (Trade Union newspaper) refers to the revolution as " a great mass movement ".

December 6, 1956—
Nepakarat states : " It is no wonder the masses, who were denied every possibility of expressing their will, finally took to arms to show what they thought." Several factories surrounded by Russian troops and A.V.O. Hundreds of factory workers in the famous ' Red ' Czepel, fight Russian troops and A.V.O., as latter try to enter a factory to arrest three members of a Workers' Council. Russian tanks open

fire on unarmed demonstrators in Budapest: two killed and several wounded.

The Chairmen of the Workers' Councils at the Ganz and MAVAG factories arrested.

The Central Workers' Council (Budapest) proclaims: " The Government does not build its power on the Workers' Councils in spite of Comrade Kadar's promises . . . Members of Workers' Councils are being arrested . . . dragged from their homes during the night without investigation or hearing . . . peaceful meetings of Workers' Councils are interrupted or prevented by armed force ". The Council demands a reply to this proclamation by 8 p.m. on December 7.

December 7, 1956—
Demonstrators (workers, students, and many women) fired on in the industrial towns Pecs. Bekeskaba and Tatabanya. Widespread arrests of rank-and-file members of Workers' Councils.

No reply to the Central Workers' Council proclamation.

December 8, 1956—
10,000 people demonstrate against the arrest of two members of the Workers' Council in the mining town of Salgatarjan : 80 casualties, dead and wounded. (Coal and uranium miners were outstanding passive resisters. Output fell to less than half of what it had been before the Revolution. Many mines were flooded.)

More clashes between workers and A.V.O. in the so-called ' Communist Party stronghold ' of Czepel, due to further arrests of workers.

Strikes (unofficial) reported from all parts of the country. The first resolution passed by Kadar's ' Socialist Workers' Party ' states that Workers' Councils are " to be taken over and cleansed of unsuitable demagogues ".

Still no reply to the proclamation of the Central Workers' Council of Budapest.

December 9, 1956—
Demonstrations by workers and students in Budapest increase. The Central Workers' Council declares a 48-hour general strike to begin on December 11 " . . . in protest against the repression of workers and their freely chosen delegates ".

Martial law declared.
The Kadar government dissolves all Regional and Central Workers' Councils—but adds that it will not dissolve these in the factories and mines.

December 11, 1956—
In the town of Eger, demonstrators force the release of jailed members of the Workers' Council.

The Chairman of the Central Workers' Council (Budapest), Sandor Racs, and its secretary, Sandor Bali, are arrested.

To show Kadar and the Russians what support the Workers' Councils still enjoy among workers throughout the country, the great, historic, 48-hour General Strike begins. The response is practically unanimous.

December 12, 1956—
At Eger a large crowd of demonstrators is fired on by the police—two workers killed, some wounded. Hand grenades then thrown by the demonstrators who occupied, for a short time, a small building which housed a printing press. Revolutionary leaflets and posters are produced and distributed. *Népszabadság* commenting on the 48-hour strike, says: " A strike, the like of which has never before been seen in the history of the Hungarian workers' movement . . . " but claims it is the result of intimidation by ' counter-revolutionaries '. In Budapest, the whole electricity supply is cut off. This hadn't happened even during the thick of the recent battles. Rail and other forms of transport paralysed throughout the country. Factories at a standstill. Large numbers of Russian tanks sent into the streets of the capital. The Kadar Government empowers Summary Courts automatically to pass the death sentence on people declared ' guilty '. At Kutfej, a 23-year-old worker is sentenced to 10 years' imprisonment for having a revolver and ammunition at his home. Big house-to-house searches for arms continue—often carried out by Russian troops.

December 13, 1956—
" People in Budapest are laughing today."—Sam Russell, *Daily Worker.*

December 14, 1956—
The two-day strike, having shown its strength, ends. The Government reminds the people that all demonstrations and assemblies are ' officially ' banned. *Pravda* states that the attempted revolution in Hungary was " a fascist putsch . . . (in which) . . . the international imperialist forces, directed by certain United States circles, played the main and decisive roles ".

December 15, 1956—
Death penalty re-introduced for striking. János Soltész brought before a Court Martial in Miskolc, charged with hiding arms, and executed immediately after the trial. This is the first known execution for this offence. Jozsef Dudas, popular chairman of the Budapest Revolutionary Committee, executed. Gyula Hay and many other writers and intellectuals arrested.

Trade Unions again ' re-organised ' and a ' reliable ' leadership installed. The name ' National Council of Free Trade Unions ' is, hypocritically, retained. (See Appendix III, February 26, 1957).

December 17, 1956—
Miners give Kadar conditions for resumption of normal work. These include: formation of their own independent

committees to represent them in negotiations with the management ; withdrawal of all Russian troops ; Nagy to be Prime Minister. A spokesman added: " If the government does not accept these conditions, no work will be done in the mines even if we miners have to go begging or emigrate from our Motherland." (*The Times*, December 17, 1956).

Reported a third of the labour force at the uranium mines in Pécs had left. Another third had been declared redundant because of electrical power shortage.

December 20, 1956—
Police empowered to imprison people for six months, without trial, whom they suspect of ' threatening public safety and production '.

December 25, 1956—
Reports of many executions. Strikers being singled out and victimised to intimidate the others. Strikes do not last long in such conditions of terror.

December 26, 1956—
Gyorgy Marosán, the Social Democrat and a Minister in the Kadar Government,[90] declares that, if necessary, the Government will execute 10,000 people to prove that *they* are the real Government, and not the Workers' Councils.

December 29, 1956—
Declaration of the Hungarian Writers' Union: " We have to state with a depressed heart that the Soviet Government made a historical mistake when it stained the revolution with blood. We predict that the time will come when the great power that erred will repent. We warn everyone away from the erroneous judgment that revolution in Hungary would have annihilated the achievements of Socialism but for the interference of Soviet arms. We know that that is not true."[91] (*The Observer*, December 30, 1956).

* * *

The events chronicled for December 1956 are only some of those we have been able to check. There were reports throughout the month of armed resistance by guerillas, particularly in the Borsod region (Hungary's largest industrial area), Veszprom, Miskolc, Szambathely, Vac, Kunszentmarton, even in the hills of Buda itself. There were moreover almost daily reports of large-scale arrests, trials, sentences and executions of workers, students and intellectuals. These would often be announced by Radio Budapest as a means of intimidation.

The diary for 1957 (see Appendix III) shows that open

---

90. Marosan, together with Kadar, Apró and Münnich, disappeared the day before the second Russian attack, presumably to form a ' Government.'

91. Early in 1957, the Writers' Union was banned. So was the Union of Journalists [see entries for January 17 and 19, 1957 in Appendix III].

resistance gradually lessened. Nevertheless, strikes and demonstrations continued throughout 1958 and 1959.

Between December 1956 and December 1957 bureaucratic control was progressively tightened. Of particular significance during this period was the systematic destruction of the Workers' Councils by the Party leaders. First there was the selective arrests of Council committee members. Next, many rank-and-file members were arrested. Then the Kadar Government stated on December 9th 1956 that all regional and central Workers' Councils were dissolved, although those in individual factories and mines were tolerated for a while longer.

The intimidation worked. By early January 1957, members of Councils not yet arrested began to resign. By the middle of the year, the purpose of the Councils had been completely destroyed. The workers' own delegates had been removed and replaced by government stooges. In September 1957, Antal Apró, Deputy Premier, announced that the remaining Workers' Councils were to be replaced by Works Councils, " under the leadership of the trade unions " (a..y shop steward will know what this means !).

By the beginning of November, the Workers' Councils were being attacked by Ferenc Münnich, Minister of the Interior, as " led by class-alien elements ". It was " necessary to replace this whole set-up as soon as possible by new organisations ".

On November 17, 1957, it was officially announced that all remaining Workers' Councils were to be abolished forthwith. The very name ' Workers' Council ' now both embarrassed and infuriated the regime. The bureaucracy attempted the impossible: to expunge from the memory of the Hungarian people and from History itself the great. positive experience of working class self-administration.

Fascist
Counter-Revolution ?

"In all its bloody triumphs over the self-sacrificing champions of a new and better society, that nefarious civilisation, based upon the enslavement of labour, drowns the moans of its victims in a hue and cry of calumny, reverberated by a world-wide echo."
K. Marx. *The Civil War in France* (1871).

Despite all this, there are, even today, members of the Communist Party who still believe their leaders' propaganda that Russian troops stopped a fascist counter-revolution in Hungary. Let us nail this lie once and for all.

In the *Daily Worker* of November 10. 1956, the British Communist Party's 'theoretician', Palme Dutt, wrote: "The issue in Hungary is between the Socialist achievements of twelve years and the return to capitalism, landlordism, and Horthy fascism, as made clear to all by Cardinal Mindszenty's broadcast." What a terrible indictment this sounds of Russian-type Communism! Does Palme Dutt really mean that large sections of the Hungarian working class actually preferred capitalism? Of course this is not true.

In our account of the Hungarian Revolution we have not mentioned the release of Cardinal Mindszenty (on October 30) nor his broadcast (on November 3) which Palme Dutt refers to. This was no mistake. We did not 'forget it'. The Mindszenty broadcast was not an important feature of the Revolution. It only appears important when one looks at the 'excuses' given by the Kremlin's apologists for the massacre of November 4.

It is unnecessary to quote the whole of Mindszenty's speech. Palme Dutt and other Stalinist propagandists based their claim of a 'return to fascism' on the fiction that Mindszenty called for the restoration of the confiscated property of the Catholic Church. While ambiguity abounded in the Cardinal's phrases, none could have been interpreted as meaning this—not even when he said he wanted "a classless society based on the rule of law and democracy and also on private ownership, correctly restricted by the interests of society and justice". This sentence might have tarred Mindszenty as God's own social-democratic confusionmonger, but never as a 'fascist'.

Reactionaries of conservative or even of fascist persuasion undoubtedly took part in the Revolution. They would no doubt have taken the fullest advantage of a new, free society to air their views. But such views would have gained insignificant support. These people certainly did not start the revolution nor did they have any influence on its development. Communist propagandists throughout the world scraped the barrel and ransacked the dispatches of press correspondents, particularly those of the Right, for any scrap of information which might be used to prove their contention. Mindszenty's broadcast, coming as it did the day before the second Russian attack, was the best they could unearth.

And even here, they were forced to misrepresent what Mindszenty had said. They were also forced to maintain an eloquent silence when, on November 5, Mindszenty had to seek refuge in the *American* Embassy. What ? Were there no Hungarian ' counter-revolutionaries ' who might have sheltered the worthy priest ? So much for his influence on the Hungarian masses in revolt. On the whole, Mindszenty supported Nagy. But Nagy was not in control—the people were. The workers would not listen to Nagy. Why should they listen to Mindszenty ?

If the Hungarian Revolution of October-December 1956 was the work of ' reactionary, fascist, counter-revolutionary forces ', where was the bureaucracy's much-vaunted ' efficiency ' ? What were the Hungarian state-security forces (A.V.O.) doing during the preparations for the uprising ? How is it no inkling of the plans for revolt ever reached the big flapping ears of the secret police ? In a state where a dossier was kept of every person above the age of six, the sort of organisation essential to a fascist, or just a plain capitalist-inspired, revolt was impossible. It may seem paradoxical, but the strength of the Hungarians in revolution lay in their lack of a centralised and bureaucratic ' revolutionary ' organisation—an organisation, that is, similar to that of their rulers.

What professional revolutionaries would have wasted valuable time in pulling down the massive statue of Stalin, in burning books and papers in the ' Horizont ' Russian bookshops, in the interminable discussions that went on in the Councils, committees, and even in the streets ?

But on the other hand, what professional revolutionaries would have been able to extract from the Hungarian working class the depths of initiative, resistance and self-sacrifice they were to show in a cause they felt to be their very own ?

The Stalinists still insist that the revolutionaries did not get their arms from the factories or from soldiers in the Hungarian army. All their propaganda at the time stressed that arms were being smuggled to the people across the Austrian border. How could the frontier guards (a section of the bureaucracy's most faithful servants, the A.V.O.) be so feckless in their ' duties ' as to allow hundreds of thousands of rifles, machine-guns, grenades—not to mention hundreds of tons of ammunition—to pass unnoticed through the electrified barbed wire and from there to proceed, unmolested, to various pre-arranged distribution points? Little more need be said about the charge of ' fascist counter-revolution '.

But there were other, minor features which, the Stalinists claim, were ' reactionary ': the demand for parliamentary elections, the illusions in U.N.O., the dropping of the term of address ' comrade '. the adoption of the word ' friend ', and the elimination of the Communist Party emblem from the Hungarian flag.

We have already commented on some of these points. The first two demands arose as the result of ten years of Stalinist rule. Not only were parties of the Right suppressed, but also all political tendencies and ideas among the working class itself. Compared with the conditions that prevailed in Russian-dominated Hungary, many of the political institutions in the West appeared as paragons of democratic virtue. Even within the ranks of the Party, all opposition was strangled. Defectors from the party line were dealt with by the security police.

It is not relevant here to make a detailed analysis of fascism. It is enough to point out that fascism had no chance among workers as politically conscious as the Hungarians showed themselves to be in October-November 1956. Moreover, the social and economic conditions essential for the growth of fascist tendencies simply do not develop under conditions of total bureaucratic capitalism. Despite this, the Party propagandists formulated a new dogma following Kadar's return from Moscow, in March 1957. They declared that " the dictatorship of the proletariat, if overthrown, cannot be succeeded by any form of government other than fascist counter-revolution ". Like in the Catholic Church, things are proclaimed as dogma which the leaders want the masses to accept but can't logically convince them of. Anyway, even before the Revolution the proletariat did *not* dictate. It was dictated *to*. And it was against this that the proletariat rose. Kadar himself was to admit all this quite explicitly when he proclaimed: " the regime is aware that the people do not always know what is good for them. It is therefore the duty of the leadership to act, not according to the *will* of the people, but according to what the leadership knows to be in the best *interests* of the people ".[92]

At the 10th Congress of the Russian Communist Party, in 1921, while the workers and sailors of Kronstadt were being ruthlessly suppressed, Trotsky had first clearly formulated the same idea. Denouncing the workers' opposition

---

92. See also other extracts from Kadar's speech to the National Assembly in Appendix III [May 10-11, 1957].

inside his own Party he explained: " They have come out with dangerous slogans ! They have made a fetish of democratic principles ! They have placed the workers' right to elect representatives above the Party. As if the Party were not entitled to assert its dictatorship even if that dictatorship temporarily clashed with the passing moods of the workers' democracy ". Trotsky spoke of the " revolutionary historical birthright of the Party." " The Party is obliged to maintain its dictatorship . . . regardless of temporary vacillations, even in the working class . . . The dictatorship does not base itself at every given moment on the formal principle of a workers' democracy . . . "

Over seventy years earlier Marx had spoken of the emancipation of the working class being the task of the working class itself. In 1921 and in 1956 Bolshevism and Stalinism respectively set out to prove him wrong. The Party leaders, not the masses, were now the embodiment of social progress. If necessary the ' temporary vacillations of the working class ' were to be corrected with Party bullets !

Why?

"All political struggles are class struggles, and all class struggles for emancipation . . . turn ultimately on the question of economic emancipation."
F. Engels. *Ludwig Feuerbach and the End of Classical German Philosophy* (1888).

"Terror implies mostly useless cruelty perpetrated by frightened people in order to reassure themselves."
F. Engels. *Letter to Marx* (September 4, 1870).

It is still not known for certain how many people lost their lives during the Hungarian Revolution. Estimates range from 20,000 to 50,000 Hungarians and from 3,500 to 7,000 Russians. The number wounded was very much higher. Since November 1956, many thousands have been executed. The number imprisoned runs into tens of thousands—most of the political prisoners released during the Revolution were later rounded up.

Some people have been aware, for a long time, of the true character of the Russian regime and of th᷾ counter-revolutionary role played by its agents (the Stalinist parties) in the working class struggles of the previous thirty years. Some remember the pitiless way the Party repressed all working class opposition within the U.S.S.R., and the sufferings it inflicted on whole populations, deported at the time of collectivisation.[93] It nevertheless seemed incredible that, before the shocked gaze of workers and Communists in every country, the Russian bureaucracy should have assumed responsibility for crushing with thousands of tanks an insurrection which had mobilised every section of the Hungarian people, and particularly the youth and the working class.

The Krushchevs, the Mikoyans, the Bulganins, had accused Stalin of every evil of the past. They had claimed to be impotent spectators of a terror they abhored. For the preceding few months they had been cavorting around the capitals of the world exhibiting themselves as 'decent chaps'. But they were guilty of a crime which matched any of Stalin's previous atrocities.

---

93. Confirmed by Krushchev at the 20th Congress.

Why did the Kremlin decide to crush Hungary?

We have examined the ' official ' excuse: Nagy was powerless to stop a fascist counter-revolution. Nagy was certainly powerless. But powerless to check the workers! For the Russians to admit this would be to admit the failure of their Communism. That is why Mao Tse-Tung, Tito, Gomulka, indeed the whole Communist hierarchy throughout the world, whatever their other differences,[94] all supported the Kremlin line. The Russian bureaucracy could find compromises with the Tildys, the Kovacs, even the Mindszentys. It could still govern by making concessions. Indeed, this had already been done, not only in Hungary, but in all the so-called ' Peoples' Democracies '. BUT THERE WAS NO BASIS WHATEVER FOR COMPROMISE WITH THE AUTONOMOUS ORGANISATIONS OF THE WORKING CLASS IN ARMS (THE COUNCILS). THEIR VICTORY WOULD HAVE SPELLED TOTAL DEFEAT FOR THE BUREAUCRACY!

Some have said Russia had no alternative but to keep Hungary well within its grip, for to withdraw would have left her vulnerable from the West. Militarily, this argument is false. Whereas Poland and East Germany were vital, Hungary and Rumania were not. It is reported that Krushchev himself had been considering the evacuation of Hungary. He believed this would have meant an immense gain in prestige. But this was *before* the Revolution.

Others have said that Eden's barbarous attack on Egypt (on November 1, 1956) greatly influenced the Kremlin's decision to launch the second attack against the Hungarians (on November 4). Because of the Suez venture, the United States propagandists were unable to exploit the Hungarian tragedy to the full. But although this was a coincidence of great convenience to the Kremlin, it is simply not true that it basically influenced their decision. The build-up of Russian armour in north-east Hungary had been going on for several days before Eden announced his ultimatum to Egypt.

Between October 23 and November 4, the working people of Hungary had spontaneously organised their own power through their Councils. To these Councils they immediately gave the greatest possible extension. These autonomous groups had formed, with extraordinary speed, a military force capable of momentarily neutralising the Russian army and the A.V.O., if not of actually compelling them to retreat. Their demands had resulted in a radical change of the workers' position within the framework of industry. They had attacked exploitation at its very roots. Public order, *their* order, had been maintained. The distribution of food, fuel and medical supplies, had been carried out magnificently. Even a reporter of *The Observer* recognised this: "A fantastic

---

94. The Chinese Communists now reproach the Russians with not having acted vigorously enough in suppressing the Hungarian Revolution !

aspect of the situation is that although the general strike is in being and there is no centrally-organised industry, the workers are nevertheless taking upon themselves to keep essential services going, for purposes which they themselves determine and support. Workers' Councils in industrial districts have undertaken the distribution of essential goods and food to the population, in order to keep them alive. The coal miners are making daily allocations of just sufficient coal to keep the power stations going and supply the hospitals in Budapest and other large towns. Railwaymen organise trains to go to approved destinations for approved purposes . . . " (November 25, 1956).

The network of Workers' and Peasants' Councils which sprang up spontaneously was the biggest single gain of the Hungarian Revolution. This was the great historical significance of Hungary '56. This has immortalised the Hungarian people. By the end of October, government by Workers' Councils was virtually a fact. This is the simple yet powerful truth that evaded so many at the time—and since.

In their decision to crush this little country, the Kremlin's logic was cold, consistent and ruthless. They could not tolerate, on their very doorstep, a country in which ordinary people were, for the first time in history, running their own affairs and were moreover advancing, in giant steps, towards genuine equality. It could not be tolerated because of the example it would have given to the other oppressed ' satellite ' peoples already seething with discontent. To allow the Revolution to triumph meant to allow its influence to be felt and acted upon by the working class of Czechoslovakia, Rumania and Yugoslavia. The workers in these countries were suffering exploitation similar to that from which the Hungarians had freed themselves. To allow the Revolution to develop would have meant giving an immense impetus to the movement in Poland which for a month had extracted concession after concession from the Polish bureaucracy as well as from the Kremlin.

Finally, Revolution in Hungary could not be tolerated because of the example it might set to the great subject people on its north-eastern borders—in the Soviet Union itself. That Russian soldiers were handing over weapons to Hungarian revolutionaries (and, in some cases, actually joining their ranks) must have chilled the spines of Krushchev and his henchmen. If sections of the Red Army proved unreliable in putting down a ' foreign ' uprising, how would the army react to a similar uprising in Russia itself. Of such stuff were nightmares made !

The Meaning of The Hungarian Revolution

> " The emancipation of the workers contains universal human emancipation — and it contains this because the whole of human servitude is involved in the relation of the worker to production. Every relation of servitude is but a modification and consequence of this relation."
> K. Marx. *Economic and Philosophic Manuscripts* (1844).

When the Hungarians were finally crushed, the Western crocodile began to weep. But it leered as it wept.

We have already seen how, in the West, ' political ' comment was centred upon the nationalistic aspects of the Revolution, no matter how trivial. Why were Western politicians so selective in their support and so parsimonious in their praise for Hungary's October ? Basically because they were opposed both to its methods and to its aims.

" The view prevailing among United States officials was that ' evolution ' towards freedom in Eastern Europe would be better for all concerned than ' revolution ', though nobody was saying this publicly ", wrote the *New York Times* (October 27, 1955). And as to ends, can anyone imagine the President of the United States, the House of Representatives, the British Prime Minister, Her Majesty's Government, Her Majesty's Loyal Opposition, the T.U.C.'s General Secretary or Her Majesty's trade union leadership supporting the fundamental social, economic and political aims of the Hungarian Revolution ? What capitalist government could genuinely support a people demanding ' workers' management of industry ' and already beginning to implement this on an increasing scale ? Such governments might go to war to protect their own class interests. One cannot conceive of them going to war to protect the interests of a Revolution which showed every sign of making both them and their bureaucratic counterparts in the East redundant. For, as Peter Fryer wrote, the Hungarian Revolution showed " the ability of ordinary working men and women to take their affairs into their own hands and manage them without a special caste of officials ".[95]

---

95. Peter Fryer, *Hungarian Tragedy.*

Naive observers could not understand why the West, having 'failed' to take a military initiative over Hungary, did not at least make some political gesture. Shocked noises they made, in UNO and elsewhere. But an effective political initiative involved supporting, clarifying and propagating the most important demands of the Hungarian workers, those that were the mainspring of the Revolution, in particular the demand without which it would not have been a people's revolution at all: *Workers' Power*—a complete change in the relations of production.

" The relations of production (boss-worker ; manager-managed ; order-giver—order-taker) remain the basis of the class structure of any society. In all countries of the world these relations are capitalist relations because they are based on wage labour."[96] The Hungarian working class attempted to transcend class society by striking at the very roots of the social system.

Certain Western observers thought their methods 'chaotic'. They deplored their ' absence of organisation '. But the Hungarian workers had instinctively grasped, although perhaps not explicitly proclaimed, that they must break completely with those traditional organisational forms which had for years entrapped both them and the working class of the West. This was their strength. They saw that it meant breaking with those very institutions which they themselves had originally created for their emancipation, and which had later become fetters upon them. New organs of struggle were created: the Workers' Councils which embodied, in embryo, the new society they were seeking to achieve. Western ' observers ' could hardly be expected to recognise all this, or to elaborate on this theme !

The working class of Western Europe, although stirred by the struggle of their Hungarian comrades, remained passive. Yet, they alone had the power to save the Revolution. They stood and watched because they were (and still are) under the ideological influence of the ' leaderships ' of ' their own ' organisations. The degeneration of these organisations is not due to ' bad leaders ' who ' betray '. " The problem has much deeper roots . . . The political and trade union organisations of the working class have increasingly adopted the objectives, methods, philosophy and patterns of organisation of the very society they were trying to supersede. There has developed within their ranks an increasing division between leaders and led, order-givers and order-takers. This has culminated in the development of a working class bureaucracy which can neither be removed nor controlled. This bureaucracy pursues objectives of its own."[97] Once this is perceived and acted upon the days of the bureaucracy will be numbered.

---

96. Quoted from *Socialism or Barbarism* [*Solidarity* pamphlet No. 11, p.3].
97. *Ibid*, pp.13-14.

In the organisation of their Workers' Councils and in the reorganisation of their trade unions, the Hungarians had shown an awareness of the fact that " the revolutionary organisation will not be able to fight the tendency towards bureaucracy unless it functions itself according to the principles of proletarian democracy and in a consciously anti-bureaucratic manner."[98] The various Councils that sprang up all over the country had the greatest possible autonomy. As far as we have been able to discover, no one ever questioned the principle that delegates elected to the Central Councils should be revocable, at all times. The principle became an immediate reality, automatically accepted and acted upon.

The massacre of the Hungarian people, the destruction of the organisations they had built during their brief spell of freedom and the re-imposition of total bureaucratic control over all aspects of their lives brought an end to an era: the era during which the Russian bureaucracy had partly succeeded—despite Stalin—in passing themselves off as defenders of Socialism and as champions of the working class. Now it would never be the same again !

The Hungarian Revolution of October 1956, wrote its message in the blood of thousands of ordinary working people, particularly the youth. The message is that, today, the class struggle throughout the world is not one between East and West, between Labour and Tory, or between employers and trade union leaders. It is the struggle of the working class for *its own* emancipation. It is the struggle of the working class against *all* the bureaucratic regimes, institutions and ideologies, which, in both East and West, obstruct its road to freedom.

Whatever we choose to call the new society we aspire to—the classless society in which men are truly free to develop to the full, and to manage all aspects of their lives—its establishment will depend on several essentials. It will depend on a different and entirely new attitude to ' leadership ' from that prevailing in the traditional organisations of the ' left ' today. It will depend on an understanding that the objective of the Revolution is not just a change in the formal ownership of property but the abolition of all special strata in society, managing the activities of others from the outside. It will depend finally on the realisation. by working people, of their ability to manage society and of the urgent need for them to do so. Without this no progress can be made towards solving the gigantic problems that confront humanity, not least of which is whether tomorrow will ever dawn or whether at any moment we shall all be destroyed in a nuclear holocaust.

Famous intellectuals have written learned books about the

---

98. *Ibid*, p.20.

world's problems in an age when life on earth could be wiped out by the decisions and actions of infinitesimal minorities. Because of their particular position within society few of these intellectuals have dared to speak out and to proclaim that the solution to these problems implies a profound social revolution in which the working people, the vast majority of mankind, will take power into their own hands and proceed to build a society where they are masters of their fate. They must do this themselves and cannot delegate the task to anybody. Real freedom depends on the extent to which this revolutionary task is both understood and acted upon.

Appendix I

Resolution of the Writers' Union
(*read to the crowd at the Bem statue, October 23, 1956*)

" We have arrived at an historic turning point. We shall not be able to acquit ourselves well in this revolutionary situation unless the entire Hungarian working people rallies round us in discipline. The leaders of the Party and the State have so far failed to present a workable programme. The people responsible for this are those who, instead of expanding Socialist democracy, are obstinately organising themselves with the aim of restoring the Stalin and Rakosi regime of terror in Hungary. We, Hungarian writers, have formulated these demands of the Hungarian nation in the following seven points :

(1) We want an independent national policy based on the principle of Socialism. Our relations with all countries, and with the U.S.S.R. and the People's Democracies in the first place, should be regulated on the basis of the principle of equality. We want a review of inter-State treaties and economic agreements in the spirit of the equality of national rights. (This was a clear reference to the uranium mines at Pecs—discovered eighteen months earlier. The Russians called them ' bauxite mines '. A.A.)

(2) An end must be put to national minority policies which disturb friendship between the people. We want true and sincere friendship with our allies—the U.S.S.R. and the Peoples' Democracies. This can be realised only on the basis of Leninist principles.

(3) The country's economic position must be clearly stated. We shall not be able to emerge from this crisis unless all workers, peasants and intellectuals can play their proper part in the political, social and economic administration of the country.

(4) Factories must be run by workers and specialists. The present humiliating system of wages, norms, social security conditions, etc., must be reformed. The trade unions must be the true representatives of the interests of the Hungarian working class.

(5) Our peasant policy must be put on a new basis. Peasants must be given the right to decide their own fate, freely. The political and economic conditions for free membership in the co-operatives must be created. The present system of deliveries to the State and of tax payment must be gradually replaced by a system ensuring free Socialist production and exchange of goods.

(6) If these points are to materialise, there must be changes of structure and of personnel in the leadership of the Party and the State. The Rakosi clique, which is seeking restoration, must be removed from our political life. Imre Nagy, a pure and brave Communist, who enjoys the confidence of the Hungarian people, and all those who have systematically fought for Socialist democracy in recent years, must be given the posts they deserve. At the same time, a resolute stand must be made against all counter-revolutionary attempts and aspirations.

(7) The evolution of the situation demands that the Peoples' Patriotic Front should assume the political representation of the working strata of Hungarian society. Our electoral system must correspond to the demands of Socialist democracy. The people must elect their representatives in Parliament, in the Council, and in *all* autonomous organs of administration, freely and by secret ballot."

Appendix II

Brief History of Personalities

Ernö Gerö, imprisoned in 1919, after the fall of the Kun regime. Fought in Spain from 1936 until the Republican collapse. Went to Moscow and became a Russian citizen. After World War II he returned to Hungary and led the Party until his friend, Rakosi, arrived.

Janos Kadar was born in 1910. His parents were farm workers. He had little education and became a locksmith. At nineteen, he joined the youth movement of the illegal Communist party. Served several short terms of imprisonment. Under the Communist regime after the war, he was made a police officer. His rise in the hierarchy was then rapid. After the merger of the communist and socialist parties, he was made a member of the Politbureau. Two months later he became Minister of the Interior. But in mid 1950 he was dismissed. Nine months later he was re-elected to the Central Committee and the Politbureau. Shortly after this he ' disappeared '.

Bela Kun was a prisoner of war in Russia during World War I. He was released by the Bolsheviks and took part in the Revolution. Author of *The Second International in Dissolution, Marxism versus Social Democracy, Lenin on the I.L.P.*: published in English by Modern Books Ltd.

Pál Maléter was an officer of the regular army during the inter-war years. In World War II, he was one of Horthy's highly-trusted personal guards until 1943, when he was sent to the Russian Front. He was taken prisoner and soon after joined a Russian-organised brigade of partisans. After a six-months' course he was made commander of a partisan group. In 1944, he parachuted into northern Hungary and fought the Nazis until Russian troops arrived. He rejoined the Hungarian Army in 1945 with the rank of major and then joined the Communist Party. When the Republic was proclaimed in 1946, Maléter was made a lifeguard of its President, Zoltan Tildy. Tildy was arrested in 1948, and Maléter rejoined the regular army. In 1951 he was promoted colonel and put in command of an armoured division. He also was given the task of training all armoured divisions including the training of officer-cadets at the school in Tata. In 1952, he was moved to the Ministry of Defence and at the end of the year he was given the post of Commander of the Works Brigades.

Imre Nagy was born in 1896, of Calvinist peasants. He had an elementary education, but became a professor in both Rostov and Budapest and a member of the Hungarian

Academy. In 1915 he was conscripted into the Army. Later taken prisoner by the Russians.

He saw the Revolution and joined the Russian Communist Party in 1918. Returned to Hungary in 1921 and worked underground against the Horthy regime. In 1927 he was arrested, but escaped to Austria a year later. He went back to Russia in 1930 and became a Russian citizen. On his return to Hungary in 1944, he became a founder-member of the 'new' regime.

Laszlo Rajk was born in 1909, in Transylvania. His father was a cobbler. He joined the Communist Party when a student at Budapest University. At the age of 23, he was imprisoned for his part in a 'Communist conspiracy' at the University. Released and worked for some time as a manual labourer. Fought in the International Brigade, in Spain, and was severely wounded in 1937. At the end of the Spanish Civil War he tried to get back to Hungary, via France, but was interned. He escaped from France in 1941, tried to enter Hungary but was arrested and imprisoned. When released he became secretary of the underground Communist Party section in Budapest. Captured by the Germans in 1944 and sentenced to death. The sentence was not carried out, but he was sent to the notorious jail of Sopronköhida and later to a concentration camp in Germany.

After his return to Hungary, at the end of the war, he became Minister of the Interior and was soon dreaded and hated for his ruthless violence. He was arrested on the orders of his 'comrades' in May 1949. His trial began on September 16, 1949. The main charge was that he had been spying for Tito's secret police. But he was also charged with spying for the American F.B.I. and for the Gestapo, with "attempting to overthrow the democratic order of Hungary", with war crimes, sedition, conspiracy, and a host of other charges. He pleaded guilty and was hanged.

Matyas Rakosi was born in 1892. His father was a poultry merchant. When young he decided on a career in the Austro-Hungarian Consular Service. Went to London to perfect his English and worked as a bank clerk. Returned to Hungary just before the outbreak of World War I, joined the Army, got a commission, was sent to the Russian front and was taken prisoner. As a P.O.W. he became an ardent supporter of the Bolsheviks. It is said that he met Lenin in 1918 and that they became friendly. Returned to Hungary in 1918 and worked with Bela Kun. When the Kun Government collapsed, he fled to Austria where he worked for the Comintern.

In 1924 he returned to Hungary to reorganise the Communist Party. For this he was soon arrested by Horthy's police and was sentenced to death. This caused uproar from certain circles in the West and as a result the sentence was commuted to eight years' imprisonment. He was released in 1935, but was later re-arrested and tried for his part in the 1919 revolution. At his trial he gained a reputation throughout the world for being fearless and outspoken. He and his lawyer—Rustem Vémbéry—used the dock with great skill to accuse the Horthy regime. In doing so, they showed a courage rarely seen in Fascist countries. This was particularly remarkable in Rakosi, who had already spent more than ten years in some of Hungary's worst prisons. He was sentenced to life imprisonment.

Following the Hitler-Stalin pact, the Horthy regime agreed to send Rakosi (and Zoltan Vas) to Russia in exchange for some flags captured by the Russians in 1849. Rakosi became a close ' friend ' of Stalin which added greatly to his 'standing' in the Communist hierarchy.

During World War II, Rakosi organised the indoctrination of Hungarian P.O.W.s and was in charge of Russian radio propaganda to Hungary. He was a naturalised Russian when he returned to Hungary with his Mongolian wife after the war. In Hungary he became one of the most ruthless tyrants of history. Copied Stalin's personality myth-building methods, and was always referred to as " our father and great master, Stalin's greatest Hungarian pupil ". On August 11, 1963, Communist Party headquarters in Budapest reported that Rakosi had recently died in Russia.

Appendix III
Diary for 1957

January 1, 1957—
In a New Year message, Miklos Samogyi, President of the recently ' re-organised ' National Council of Free Trade Unions, appeals to the miners: " Miners, we beg of you to give us more coal ! " The miners gave ' them ' more coal—more coal left in the pits !

January 3, 1957—
The miners of Tatabanya (production since the second Russian attack cut to 3% of normal) again out on strike, this time in protest against the arrest of 12 brother miners. *Népszabadság* reports ' large quantities ' of arms and ammunition found hidden in a pitshaft entrance, in the mining town of Várpolata.

January 4, 1957—
A military court sentences a 25-year-old transport worker to death for being in illegal possession of arms on October 30, 1956—i.e., before the Kadar Government even existed !

January 5, 1957—
After a visit to Budapest, N. S. Krushchev states : " In Hungary, everything is now in order."

January 6, 1957—
Kadar issues statement on the ' major tasks ' of the Government: " Russian troops will remain in Hungary for the time being, in order to repel the whole imperialist attack . . . The question of their withdrawal will be a matter of negotiations between the U.S.S.R. and Hungary." The statement hailed the establishment of the Workers' Councils as " one of the great achievements of the regime ", but in future, their function was to be changed slightly. They were to ensure that " the workers adhere strictly to Government decisions ". Due to severe intimidation, with many of their comrades arrested and some believed to have been already executed, members of Workers' Councils now begin to resign.

January 8, 1957—
The Central Workers' Council of Czepel resigns and issues the following statement :
" It was the hallowed events of the October 23 Revolution of the Hungarian people that brought us into being so that we could build an independent, free and democratic Hungary, and establish the basis for a way of life free from fear.

" The events that have taken place in the meantime, however, have prevented us from fulfilling our mandate. We are to have no other role than to carry out the orders of the Government. We cannot carry out orders that oppose our mandate. We cannot sit passively when members of Workers' Councils are being arrested and harassed, and when the entire work of the Workers' Councils is branded as 'counter-revolutionary'. For these reasons, and regardless of our personal fate, we have unanimously decided to resign our mandate.

"Our decision does not mean that we are trying to evade responsibility. It is our opinion that our continued existence would help to deceive our comrades. We therefore return our mandate to the workers."

January 9, 1957—
Industrial troubles, strikes and demonstrations, flare up more violently in all parts of the country.

January 10, 1957—
Workers demonstrate in Czepel against the installation of a Government Commissioner and a director in the engineering works. The militia, reinforced by Russian troops, is called in. Workers dispersed after three hours of fighting. Situation in Czepel so grave that Government issues order forbidding newspaper reporters to visit island.

January 11, 1957—
Official statement issued that one killed and six injured in 'disturbances' at the Czepel engineering works.

January 13, 1957—
Official announcement over radio that, due to continuing 'counter-revolutionary' activity in industry, Summary Courts to be given additional power to impose the death sentence for almost any act against the Kadar Government. In addition to the death sentence for anyone calling a strike, the new decree declares it illegal for workers even to *discuss* possible strike action.

January 15, 1957—
"The Central Council of the Hungarian Workers has issued a manifesto addressed to the workers. It says that against the terror of the Russian rulers, assisted by their Hungarian henchmen, there is only one thing to be done—to fight to the bitter end. It is a question of 'to be or not to be' the statement adds. Because of the terror, however, and the death penalty even for distributing leaflets, the Council exhorts the workers to spread all news concerning the underground by word of mouth. Sabotage and passive resistance are the order of the day. Strikes and go-slow tactics are recommended." (*The Times*).

January 17, 1957—
The Writers' Union dissolved by decree.

January 19, 1957—
The Union of Journalists dissolved by decree.
Janos Szabo, the elderly worker who played a prominent

part in the Szena Square battles, executed.

January 21, 1957—
" The waves of arbitrary arrests continue. Hundreds of members of Revolutionary Councils are in prison. During the last week there have been a number of judges who have resigned in protest against what they called the farce of this jurisdiction." (*The Times*).

January 25, 1957—
Statement by the Ministry of Interior (over Budapest Radio) that the writers Gyula Hay, Domokos Varga, Tibor Tardos, Zoltan Roth and Balazs Lengyel, and the journalists Sandor Novobaczky and Pal Letay, have been arrested and charged with participating in ' counter-revolutionary ' activities.

January 27, 1957—
Police announce that another 35 people have been arrested today in Budapest. Minister of State, Marosán, declares that " the insurrection was organised by international imperialism ".

January 29, 1957—
In a speech to the ' trade unions ', Kadar says he has " never relied on his Government being popular with the Hungarian people ".
Radio Budapest announces that the Government has ' suspended ' the activity of the Workers' Council of Railwaymen.

February 3, 1957—
Marosán repeats the threats he made at the end of December: the Government " will create a climate of terror for the enemies of the people ".

February 5, 1957—
Discussions between the public prosecutors, the Minister of State (Marosán) and the Minister of the Interior (Münnich). Decision to introduce new measures aimed at " the restoration of discipline and public order ". The amnesty promised by Kadar on November 4 for all ' counter-revolutionaries ' who laid down their arms is withdrawn. (Only very few people had been taken in. They had paid for their gullibility with their lives.)

February 13, 1957—
Newspapers celebrate the 12th anniversary of Russian troops' entry into Budapest.

February 18, 1957—
One of Kadar's promises, given at the meeting with workers' delegates on November 17, is to be fulfilled. A " workers' militia " is to be established . . . for the purpose of " maintaining discipline among the workers ".

February 21, 1957—
Bela Barta, accused of " organising demonstrations on December 10, as a result of which people were killed and

118

injured " (by Kadar's police !) is sentenced to 14 years' imprisonment by a tribunal at Miskolc.

February 21-23, 1957—
Violent clashes between workers and police, sparked off by re-erection of red stars over industrial plants in Budapest.

February 26, 1957—
Beginning of two-day conference of the ' Provisional Central Committee ' of the Socialist Workers' Party. In a long resolution, part of the section dealing with how the unions are to ' serve ' the workers, states: " We reject as reactionary the demand that trade unions should be independent of both the Party and the Workers' and Peasants' Government, and the demand for the right to strike in defiance of the Workers' State ".

March 5, 1957—
Gyula Kallai, Minister of Culture, declares that a " systematic ideological propaganda is necessary to liberate the intellectuals from counter-revolutionary influences ".

March 6, 1957—
A new literary weekly *Magyarosag* is published in Budapest to replace *Irodalmi Ujsag* (literary gazette of the dissolved Writers' Union). It announces the formation of new literary club, Tancsis, to replace the Petőfi Circle.

March 17, 1957—
Announcement that a Communist Youth organisation is to be formed.

March 20, 1957—
Ministry of Interior issues order that persons " dangerous to the State or to public security " are liable to " forced residence " at places specified by the authorities.

March 23, 1957—
Minister of State, Marosán, states at a meeting in Czepel that Russian troops will remain in Hungary " as long as the interests of the workers require their presence ".

March 27, 1957—
At a press conference, Marosán declares that " although the counter-revolutionaries have suffered defeat . . . some disturbing elements still remain to be eliminated ".

April 8, 1957—
At a trial in Budapest, three of the accused are sentenced. Playwright, Joseph Gali, and journalist, Gyula Obersovsky, charged with publishing an illegal journal and ' agitation ', are sentenced to 1 and 3 three years respectively. (But see below: June 20, 25 and July 4).

April 17, 1957—
Radio Budapest announces that " counter-revolutionary " Miklos Olach, aged 21, has been executed at Borsod for " killing an officer of the Hungarian Army ".

119

April 20, 1957—
Ministry of Interior issues a communiqué that the writer, Tibor Dery, has been arrested and charged with "behaviour prejudicial to the security of the State ".

April 29, 1957—
Announcement that Minister of State, Marosán, has been appointed First Secretary of the Budapest section of the ' Socialist Workers' Party '.

May 1, 1957—
In a May Day speech, Marosán pays tribute to Kadar for " creating the conditions that have made possible the existence of the Party and of socialist Hungary ".

May 3, 1957—
The trade union paper *Nepakarat* reports the arrest of a " counter-revolutionary band " of nine workers in the Nograd area. They are accused of obstructing Russian tanks from entering the industrial town of Solgotorjan.

May 10-11, 1957—
Meeting of National Assembly. Kadar says: " The task of the leaders is not to put into effect the wishes of the masses . . . the leaders' task is to realise the interests of the masses . . . In the recent past, we have encountered the phenomenon of certain categories of workers acting against their own interests . . . If the wishes of the masses do not coincide with progress, then they must be led in another direction."

June 20, 1957—
Announcement that Joseph Gali and Gyula Obersovsky have now been sentenced to death. Other prison sentences of accused in the same trial are raised.

June 25, 1957—
Official communiqué announces the re-trial of the writers Gali and Obersovsky. In the meantime, death sentences suspended.

June 27, 1957—
National Conference of the ' Socialist Workers' Party ' opens in Budapest. Kadar gives a report on the general situation—couples Nagy with Rakosi as " guilty of treason ".

June 29, 1957—
National Conference ends. A resolution condemning the " counter-revolution attempt of October-November 1956 " admits that it is not yet defeated : " Those who have committed crimes and continue to undermine the people's regime, will be severely punished ". Tribute is paid to " the brotherly help of the Soviet Union ".

July 4, 1957—
Death sentences on Gali and Obersovsky quashed by the Budapest Supreme Court. They are sentenced instead to life and fifteen years' imprisonment respectively.

July 9, 1957—
Népszabadság reports that police had to be called in to put an end to strike of building workers which started on June 5, at Sajoszent-Peter, for a wages increase.

July 25, 1957—
In a speech, Minister of State, Marosán, says hundreds of arrests made during recent weeks . . . also that the Soviet Union has agreed to the Hungarian Government's request that Rakosi should remain in exile in the U.S.S.R.

August 7, 1957—
Announcement that there is to be a trial of seven workers who have been charged with " counter-revolutionary " activities in the Tatabanya coalfields, where strikes and " industrial unrest " continue.

August 20, 1957—
Purge of schoolteachers in Miskolc.
Nepakarat reports speech by Sandor Gaspar, Secretary of the ' Council of Free Trade Unions ', during which he said: " Absenteeism, unpunctuality and unjustified early departure from work, have increased in factories during the last months ".

September 1, 1957—
Third volume of the official *White Book* published in Budapest. This gives the total number of ' comrades ' killed during the revolution as 201 (166 members of the A.V.O., 26 Party officials—including people working for the A.V.O.—and 9 civilians).
Celebrating ' Miners' Day ' at Tatabanya, Kádar admits that the " October mood " still prevails among the miners.

September 17, 1957—
Népszabadság scolds factory managers who throw on to the Government the responsibility for " tightening norms and reducing wages ", instead of " explaining that such unpopular decisions are made in the interests of the workers ".

September 21-23, 1957—
Marosán makes speeches in several parts of Budapest, including the Technical University. " If there are any demonstrations on October 23, those taking part will be severely punished." As if to add emphasis to this, he adds that 1,200 people were arrested in July.

September 29, 1957—
At Kecskemet, Deputy Premier Antal Apro announces that the remaining Workers Councils are to be replaced by " works councils, under the leadership of the trade unions ".

October 15, 1957—
Népszabadság repeats threats of heavy penalties for any person who " disturbs the peace " on October 23, and emphasises the need for " increased vigilance ".

October 16. 1957—
Marosán again warns students against any demonstrations on October 23.

October 23. 1957—
Budapest and other cities had a calm day.
A.V.O. out on the streets in great numbers.
Russian troops standing by.

November 2, 1957—
Budapest City Council decides to erect a statue of Lenin —on the pedestal at the plinth in City Park where had stood the 26 ft. bronze statue of Stalin, pulled down by demonstrators on October 23, 1956.
The Hungarian Writers' Association Abroad receives reports of a secret trial of Gyula Hay, Tibor Dery, Zoltan Zelk and Tibor Tardos.

November 3, 1957—
Writing in *Népszabadság*, the Minister of the Interior, Ferenc Münnich, reports on the first year's achievements of the Kadar Government. He attacks the Workers' Councils which " were led by class-alien elements . . . It is necessary to replace this whole set-up by new organisations as soon as possible ".

November 13, 1957—
Radio Budapest announces that the trial of the writers (held in camera since the beginning of the month) has ended. The verdict of the Supreme Court is : Tibor Dery (aged 63) sentenced to nine years' imprisonment ; Gyula Hay (57) six years ; Zoltan Zelk (51) three years ; and Tibor Tardos 18 months. Report that during the proceedings, Dery and Hay declared that if a similar situation were to arise today, they would act exactly as they did in October 1956.

November 17, 1957—
Official announcement that all remaining Workers' Councils are to be abolished forthwith.

Appendix IV

Sources of Information and Quotations

Books & Pamphlets

L. B. BAIN. *The Reluctant Satellites*, Macmillan, New York, 1960.

NOEL BARBER. *A Handful of Ashes*, Wingate, 1957.

HUGO DEWAR & DANIEL NORMAN. *Revolution and Counter-Revolution in Eastern Europe*, Socialist Union of Central Eastern Europe, 1957.

PETER FRYER. *Hungarian Tragedy*, Dobson Books Ltd., 1956.

YGAEL GLUCKSTEIN. *Stalin's Satellites in Europe*, Allen & Unwin, 1952.

ADMIRAL NICHOLAS HORTHY. *Memoirs*, Hutchinson, 1956.

The Hungarian Workers' Revolution, Syndicalist Workers Federation, 1956.

ALEXANDRA KOLLONTAI. *The Workers' Opposition*, Solidarity Pamphlet No. 7.

GEORGE MIKES. *The Hungarian Revolution*, Andre Deutsch, 1957.

ANAND MISHRA. *East European Crisis of Stalinism*, Calcutta, 1957.

HUBERT RIPKA. *Eastern Europe in the Post-war World*, Methuen, 1961.

The Road of Our People's Democracy, Hungarian News and Information Services, June 1952.

HUGH SETON-WATSON. *Eastern Europe, 1918-1941*, Cambridge, 1945.

HUGH SETON-WATSON. *The East European Revolution*, Methuen, 1950.

G. N. SHUSTER. *In Silence I Speak*, Gollancz. 1956.

Socialism or Barbarism. Solidarity Pamphlet No. 11.

Newspapers & Periodicals

Continental News Services

Daily Worker

The Economist

The Guardian

Irodalmi Ujsag (Literary Gazette)

The Nation

Nemzetör (Monthly of the Hungarian Freedom Fighters)

Nepakarat (' Official ' Hungarian T.U. newspaper)

Neue Zürcher Zeitung

New York Times

The Observer

Polish Facts and Figures

Pravda

Scanteia (Rumanian CP daily)

Socialisme ou Barbarie

Solidarity

Szabad Nep (Hungarian CP daily)

The Times

Tribune

World News and Views

Matyas Bajor and five other young Freedom Fighters were interviewed in London by the author, in January, 1957.